Active Parenting Today

For Parents of 2 to 12 Year Olds

Leader's Guide

by
Michael H. Popkin, Ph.D.

The Active Parenting Purpose

"To support the development of human potential through the family structure by providing parents with the information and skills to foster in their children the qualities necessary for thriving in a democratic society: cooperation, courage, responsibility and self-esteem."

ISBN 1-880283-04-2

Photographs by Julie Fletcher and Tom Hurst

Acknowledgements

Active Parenting Today is a major revision of the original *Active Parenting Discussion Program*, first published in 1983. Our thanks and appreciation go first to the thousands of leaders who chose this program as their resource for improving the lives of families. Your confidence in these materials, your enthusiasm and encouragement for what we are collectively doing, your letters of support and your letters of criticism were all instrumental in bringing us to this important threshold. You have made us the recognized leader in video-based parenting education, and we thank you.

Our commitment to parenting education and to parenting educators has driven us to constantly strive to create better ways for teaching the information and skills that today's parents so desperately need. Once again, we are indebted to our leaders. There is an old adage that says, "If it ain't broke, don't fix it." I believe that this way of thinking is at best a hindrance to progress and at worst a precursor of disaster. Our leaders share with us a commitment to improving things before they are broken. Even while they used the original program effectively, they encouraged us to begin research and development on the next generation of Active Parenting. The result is *Active Parenting Today*, a program that integrates the constructive feedback gleaned from over nine years of listening to some of the best parenting educators in the land.

Systematic research for this revision was carried out under the able direction of Susan Greathead, our former director of product development. She, along with Lisa Wasshausen and Nancy Ballance, interviewed 40 of the most active Active Parenting leaders in the United States and Canada. These leaders, who had collectively led over 5,000 parents through the program, were taken through a 10-page questionnaire covering every imaginable aspect of the video, the *Leader's Guide* and the *Parent's Guide*. Their input was critical in revising the program into a working draft of *Active Parenting Today*.

This information was used by me to write the draft for this revision. An advisory board comprised of 14 highly gifted and experienced leaders was then sent the video scripts and manuscripts for critique. Their suggestions were carefully reviewed by our product development team and given to me to integrate into a new draft.

This draft was then sent to a team of very skilled editors: Susan O'Halloran, who edited the video script, and Susan Palmer and Nancy Ballance, who edited the *Leader's Guide* and the *Parent's Guide*. The manuscripts were then turned into books by our staff designer, Jim Polak, who brings a bit of creativity to everything he touches. The scripts were brought to life on video under the direction of our wonderful producer/director, Maryanne Culpepper. Finally, Lisa Wasshausen assumed responsibility for the completion of the entire revision project midstream and did a superb job of bringing all the pieces together on time and in excellent form.

To all of these people, and to the now more than one million "active parents" who helped inspire them, I express my thanks and my gratitude.

Active Parenting Today Advisory Board

Gwen Aldredge, Ph.D.
College Professor
Waco, Texas

Sandy Barclay, M.Ed.
Parent Educator
Fayetteville, Arkansas

Gary Bennett
Caseworker, Juvenile Court System
Battle Creek, Michigan

Fred Bogin, M.D.
Pediatrician
Hollis, New Hampshire

Gary Evans, M.Div.
Therapist
Moreno Valley, California

Ruth Glaze, M.C.C.
Therapist
Jackson, Mississippi

Jim Granade, Ph.D.
Consultant, Prevention Resource Center
Stone Mountain, Georgia

Virgil Leopold, Ph.D.
Elementary School Principal
Monroe, Wisconsin

Mimi Lupin, M.A.
Parent Educator
Houston, Texas

Marian Michael, M.A.
High School Counselor
Golden Valley, Minnesota

Claudia Noel, M.S.
School Psychologist
Ashland, Ohio

Jane Oczkewicz, M.Ed.
Elementary School Counselor
Port Orchard, Washington

Al Reynar, M.Ed.
Parent Educator
Alberta, Canada

Jim Rider, Ph.D.
Director, Christian Family Center
Holly Ridge, North Carolina

Table of Contents

A Letter to The Leader
From Dr. Popkin

Dear Fellow Parenting Educator,

Before founding Active Parenting Publishers in 1980, I was working as a child and family therapist for a community mental health system. I had experienced firsthand, as perhaps you have, that parenting education was not just something to help so-called "high risk" families, but that teaching parents effective skills could benefit *all* families.

I also found that leading parenting groups soon became the most satisfying part of my job. Many times I would go out to lead an evening group, tired from a long day's work, only to find myself energized and revitalized at the end of a two-hour session. The enthusiasm of the parents, their stories and anecdotes about improvements at home, and their sincere gratitude to me, their leader, made me feel that I was making a valuable contribution to our community. No wonder I felt invigorated!

Still, I had a gnawing sense that we in the parenting education field could do more. Like skilled workers in any field, I felt that with better tools we could provide better services. My goal in establishing Active Parenting Publishers was to provide you with improved tools for doing this important work. The original *Active Parenting Discussion Program* (© 1983) introduced the concept of video-based training to the parenting education field. The power and ease of this advanced educational technology has helped fuel an explosion in the parenting education movement. Parenting is finally getting the support it deserves as more and more schools, religious organizations, mental health centers, hospitals, community organizations, military bases and even businesses are offering Active Parenting groups.

Thanks to leaders such as yourself, over a million parents now have participated in the *Active Parenting Discussion Program* or *Active Parenting of Teens* (© 1990). We have encouraged those leaders to stay in touch with us so that we might form a network of parenting educators who exchange information and share ideas. Our magazine, *Leader,* now serves more parenting educators than any other publication of its kind. Through this network we learned of the need for a self-esteem program for children that would complement the *Active Parenting Discussion Program*. The result was *Free the Horses*, the first video-based self-esteem curriculum. We listened to our leaders again and a year later released *Windows: Healing and Helping Through Loss*—the first video-based loss education program.

The original *Active Parenting Discussion Program* is now 10 years old, and the concepts are as relevant today as a decade ago. We took 10 years of experience as the recognized leader in the field of video-based parenting education and created *Active Parenting Today*. I am honored that you have taken the time to review this program and hope you are as excited about it as we are.

Now, a word about the *Leader's Guide*. If you are new to parenting education, you will probably want to rely heavily on this guide at first. (I've given you some time estimates throughout to help you pace your group.) As you gain experience and confidence, you will find that some of this material fits your own style better than other parts. Please do not feel you have to use this program rigidly! Pick and choose, modify, omit and otherwise improve your course as it suits you. Remember, you are the key to the success of this program.

Finally, thank you for being part of the parenting education movement. Whatever materials you use to do your work effectively, we are certainly all in this together. After all, the future of our human community rests with the children, their parents and those who support them.

Here's to your success!

Michael H. Popkin

Michael H. Popkin
Founder
Active Parenting Publishers

Why Parenting Education?

Parenting education groups are flourishing as never before. The demand for information, skills and support relating to this important—and difficult—job is increasing at an incredible rate. Schools, churches and synagogues, mental health centers and a host of professionals and para-professionals are joining an ever-growing network of parenting educators. Why? Here are some of the reasons we have heard:

- Society has changed so much in the past 30 years that the need for new parenting skills has become imperative.
- The old autocratic approach seems to foster rebellion in modern children.
- The newer permissive style also has been found wanting.
- Parents want something that works!
- With so much mobility, the informal parenting education of the extended family is missing.
- Parenting has become recognized as a skill and, like any skill, it can be improved.
- As one mother put it, "Kids don't come with instructions."

A Word About Prevention

One of the most serious concerns facing parents today is the threat of tobacco, alcohol and other drugs. The problem is real. The statistics are alarming. And when the problem hits home, the results are often devastating.

As a consultant for the United States Office of Substance Abuse Prevention (OSAP), I served on an "expert panel" that developed guidelines for a parent's role in the prevention effort. The project, which was aptly named "Parent Training Is Prevention," recommended 10 roles parents could play in the prevention of alcohol and other drug use in their children. Having written two of the position papers for OSAP on these roles, I was pleased to develop a chapter for our program *Active Parenting of Teens* on "The Challenge of Alcohol and Other Drugs." By doing so, *Active Parenting of Teens* became the first major parenting program (and as of this printing the only major parenting program), to follow OSAP's recommendation to integrate these 10 roles and other prevention information into existing parenting education materials.

Active Parenting Today focuses on children from ages 2 to 12 and continues this tradition of "parenting is prevention." While some OSAP roles are more appropriate for parents when their children reach the teen years, there's still a strong anti-drug foundation to be laid at an early age. Specifically, there are three areas in which *Active Parenting Today* works to support parents in preventing the use of tobacco, alcohol and other drugs (TAOD) in their children—now, and when they become teens:

1. To build a strong parent-child relationship.

    Styles of parenting that are either too autocratic or too permissive tend to develop rebellious children who often do the opposite of what their parents want. This not only reduces the ability of the parent to influence the child away from drugs, but can actually be a counterproductive force that further drives the child towards drugs.

    When parents learn an effective model of parenting with skills for discipline, communication, encouragement, family enrichment and problem solving, they not only develop a positive parent-child relationship, but also become equipped to guide their children towards positive choices, such as abstinence from TAOD.

2. To help parents instill in their children the fundamental "no-use" qualities of self-esteem, courage, responsibility and cooperation.

    It is widely accepted that children with high self-esteem are less likely to become involved with TAOD. Having the courage to work hard to succeed, the ability to make responsible choices, and the cooperation to work well with authority figures as well as peers are all key qualities in the "no-use" child.

    Active Parenting Today is organized around the parenting skills necessary for instilling these qualities in our children. As such, everything that parents do to develop these qualities can be viewed as solid prevention.

3. To raise parental awareness of the threat of TAOD, and to inform them of the roles they can play in the prevention process—including how to talk with their children about the subject.

    Everyone these days seems to be admonishing parents to talk with their children about TAOD. However, this is usually easier said than done. Parents who have little idea how to have such a discussion are rightly afraid they may do more harm than good. The result is that they often do nothing.

Active Parenting Today teaches parents effective communication skills that may be used in any number of situations, then models how to have a "Family Talk" using the subject of TAOD as the example.

By observing on the video how to have such a talk with their children, parents are better able to do it themselves. In addition, a special booklet, *Active Parenting Family Guide: Tobacco, Alcohol and Other Drugs,* has been developed as part of the program to assist parents at home in holding these important discussions. Finally, the 10 roles recommended by OSAP for parents to play in the prevention process are presented in the *Active Parenting Today Parent's Guide* and in this *Leader's Guide.*

As a result, *Active Parenting Today* is the first comprehensive parenting program for parents of children ages 2 to 12 to fully incorporate the latest information and skills in the prevention movement.

For What Parents Is *Active Parenting Today* Appropriate?

The skills and concepts taught in *Active Parenting Today* are within the range of almost all parents. They also have a long history of success with special populations. Some of the groups that Active Parenting leaders have worked well with include parents of deaf children, ADD children, hospitalized children and children with learning disabilities; court-ordered parents who have abused or neglected their children; parents who have been abused or neglected as children themselves; single parents; stepparents; and parents in Chapter One schools.

Active Parenting Today is effective with such diverse groups because of three factors:

1. Families are more alike than different. As such, all parents struggle with issues of discipline, communication, encouragement, problem solving and the like.
2. The skills and concepts taught are common to anyone parenting in a democratic society. They work.
3. *Active Parenting Today* leaders are able to modify the presentation of the material to better fit their particular population of parents.

In one study conducted by a county school system, parents in Chapter One schools (schools with a lower socioeconomic population and lower academic achievement level) and parents in more affluent schools both successfully completed an Active Parenting program with equally positive results.

Why a Video-Based Program?

A successful parenting education program depends as much on *how* we teach as on *what* we teach. My goal in founding Active Parenting Publishers in 1980 was to apply state-of-the-art educational technology to the field of parenting education. Three years of research and development led me to conclude that video-based training was the most cost-effective innovation available. Today this powerful delivery system continues to be the state of the art. Here's why:

- Video shows as well as tells, and behavioral modeling is a powerful learning method.
- In one study on learning attributed to Xerox, people retained:
    - 10% of what they read,
    - 20% of what they heard,
    - but 50% of what they saw!
- When integrated into a multi-sensory approach using the *Parent's Guide*, activities, video, discussion, practice and feedback, retention has been as high as 80-90%.
- This is why most Fortune 500 companies have adopted video-based training as their standard.
- Because it's more interesting, stimulating and entertaining, more parents will participate.
- A complete video-based package saves the leader preparation time that he can use in other activities.
- During group sessions the video is like a co-leader, giving the group leader a chance to relax and plan while the course is still progressing.
- Today's parents grew up on TV. They identify with the medium. They like it!

The Materials

The *Active Parenting Today* video-based package brings together the following elements to create a synergistic learning experience. That is, when used together, the total program is more powerful than its individual parts.

Leader's Guide

Anyone who attempts to replace a leader with a film or video is missing the boat. Films and videos do not train; they simply enable a leader to train more effectively. The key to an *Active Parenting Today* group is still the leader, and therefore the *Leader's Guide* is an essential element of the training package. Because the content can be more efficiently presented by the video and the *Parent's Guide*, the leader's role is to provide structure, organization and feedback. This means that an effective leader may be either an expert in the content area or a beginner—the essential qualification is only that she be an effective facilitator.

The *Leader's Guide* is divided into six chapters, one for each group session, with an additional section about leader preparation. Each chapter includes an organizer that breaks down the session into topic areas, group exercises and video scenes. This aids the leader in organizing the session and reviewing it before future sessions. The *Leader's Guide* contains questions (and examples of answers) for reviewing the video, instructions for all group activities, brief explanations to be made by the leader, and home activity assignments. It is sufficiently detailed so that a beginning leader can follow it in a step-by-step manner and lead a successful group. However, the *Leader's Guide* is just that, a guide. Leaders are encouraged to personalize their groups as their experience and expertise allow.

Video Segments

The video provides a visual presentation and demonstration of the content. It usually includes negative examples of how an autocratic or permissive ("dictator" or "doormat") parenting technique fails to handle a situation, and always models the alternative active parenting method. In some scenes colorful paintings are used to complement brief, narrated teaching stories. However, most of the 52 scenes depict five families, played by professional actors, engaged in a variety of typical family situations. Most scenes are under two minutes in length, with the longest running 8 minutes. The total video content is about 158 minutes, which spread out over six sessions is about 26 minutes per 2-hour session. These brief scenes are an ideal amount of video for a 2-hour session.

We also found that parents participating in the original *Active Parenting Discussion Program* responded particularly well to those videos in which humor was used. For this reason you'll notice several of the vignettes in each session utilize humor to drive home key points.

The video is narrated by Kevin Loring. Expert commentary is offered throughout by Dr. Michael Popkin, the program's author. These narratives and dialogues, though brief, serve to provide additional information and analysis to the group.

Video Review

In continuing to innovate the delivery of parenting information, we have developed a method of summarizing the content of each session called a "video review." Based on the idea that "a picture is worth a thousand words," and that the mind can absorb much more than the ear can hear, the video review is a montage of key information presented on the videos in each session. The video review replaces the need for a leader to summarize the material at the end of each session. This visual review allows the unconscious mind an additional opportunity to absorb and process the information presented.

Parent's Guide

The *Parent's Guide*, the other major component of the program, contains all of the information covered in *Active Parenting Today*. Although the video segments and *Leader's Guide* are designed to present the information to the group, the parents' ability to retain this information will be greatly enhanced by reading the *Parent's Guide* at home each week.

To encourage this important reading, the *Parent's Guide* is designed to be what computer enthusiasts would call "user friendly." Streamlined to just 168 pages of information, examples, charts and photographs, the two-color format with wide margins invites reading. Each of the photographs used in the *Parent's Guide* was taken during the video production. When parents review the text in the future, they will associate these pictures with the video scenes and the discussion and analysis that followed. This feature will help parents remember and apply the skills they have learned.

Also important in the *Parent's Guide* are the activity pages found at the conclusion of each chapter. Because active learning is effective learning, parents are encouraged to apply their new skills at home each week and then fill out the activity pages in the *Parent's Guide*. At the beginning of each group session, leaders provide feedback for these activities during Share And Tell time.

The Active Parenting Learning System

It is more than just the use of video that makes video-based training so much more effective than traditional delivery systems. It is video integrated into a total training package that includes at least seven separate steps. Each major topic or skill is experienced by the parent at least seven times. The repetition and interaction through various communication modes are particularly effective.

THE ACTIVE PARENTING LEARNING SYSTEM

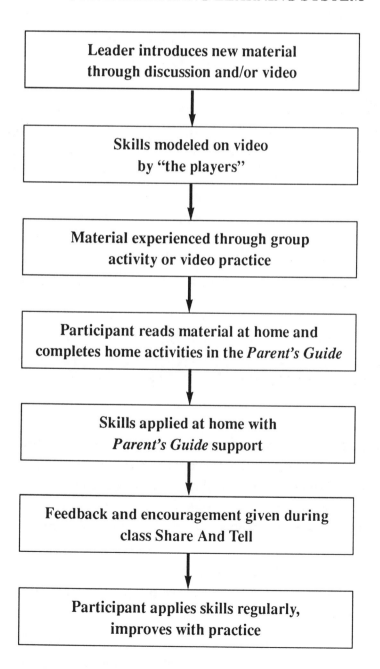

Leader introduces new material through discussion and/or video
Skills modeled on video by "the players"
Material experienced through group activity or video practice
Participant reads material at home and completes home activities in the *Parent's Guide*
Skills applied at home with *Parent's Guide* support
Feedback and encouragement given during class Share And Tell
Participant applies skills regularly, improves with practice

Who Can Lead an
Active Parenting Today Group?

Effective leaders need not be experts in the field of parenting education, as the content of the program is communicated through the video and *Parent's Guide*. Leaders range from highly experienced professionals to lay persons. The keys appear to be an ability to understand the content, good facilitation skills, an encouraging attitude, and a desire to help others improve their family life. Here are a few examples of the many types of leaders:

counselors • nurses • therapists • teachers • lay persons
clergy • physicians • training and development staff

Is Leader Training Required?

No. Active Parenting Publishers does not require that leaders receive any formal training. However, Leader Certification Workshops (LCWs) are offered throughout the United States and other parts of the world for those individuals who would like to participate in these one-day training experiences. LCW participants learn how to lead an *Active Parenting Today* or *Active Parenting of Teens* group from nationally recognized trainers, meet with fellow parenting educators, and enhance their group presentation skills. These workshops are not required by Active Parenting but remain popular with new leaders as well as with those who have taught our programs for many years.

Group Leadership Skills

Your main role as an *Active Parenting Today* leader is *not* to present the information. The *Parent's Guide* and video will do most of that. Your role is to facilitate the learning process so that your group members learn to apply the information in their own families. Some aspects of group leadership that will be helpful:

1. **Playing the videos**. Allow about 30 minutes to acquaint yourself with an unfamiliar VCR (videocassette recorder). This should be done at least several days before your first group session. During the sessions sit next to the VCR so that you can operate the controls without getting up, or use a remote control.

2. **Introducing topics**. We have designated information for you to present throughout the *Leader's Guide* in bold type. You will want to make other points as you go. Keep in mind:

   - Be brief.
   - Be prepared (don't read to your group; rehearse first).
   - Don't do all their thinking for them.

3. **Leading discussion**. The majority of each group session is spent in discussion. The *Leader's Guide* provides questions for reviewing the material, processing activities and analyzing the video. Again, you may want to include your own ideas. Some discussion skills to remember:

   - Focusing. Keep the group on the subject and help them focus on how the skill or concept is being applied.

   - Postponing. Members will often try to get you to play advisor by asking you specific questions about their children. Don't get hooked! If you begin listening to long stories about "what happened yesterday morning," you will never cover the information and skills that would enable them to handle their own problems. Remember, *Active Parenting Today* is not a rap or advice group. There are places in each chapter of the *Parent's Guide* (beginning with Chapter Two) for parents to apply the information and skills to their own situations. Postpone premature questions with something like this:

     "It sounds like you are getting into a real-life situation. Can you save it until the end of the session when we begin analyzing behavior?"

   - Inviting. You can sometimes bring quiet members into the discussion by asking them what they think. However, avoid pressure, and if they resist, back off.

   - Sidestepping the struggle for power. This is an important technique for parents to learn with rebellious children, and it is also important for leaders to learn with rebellious parents. Do not be alarmed if parents disagree with something in the program. They do not need to accept 100% in order to gain a lot from the group. Avoid direct arguments.

"Does anyone want to respond to Jerry's comment?"
"This may not be the most effective approach for you. But I think you will be in a better position to decide a little later in the course."
"You may be right. What would the author of the program have to say?"
"We have a lot of material to cover, so we had better move on for now."

- Making connections. Help the group make the connection between the concepts and skills of *Active Parenting Today* and the situations being expressed on video or in their own families.

    "I wonder if your conflict with Steven isn't a little like the conflict between Diane and Stephanie we saw in that first video."

4. **Developing group cohesiveness**. The support that parents experience in Active Parenting groups can be fostered by the leader. Some ways:

    - Find commonalities among members. After a vignette portraying a conflict, you might say,

        "How many of you have ever felt like Dad does right now?"

    - Take turns bringing refreshments so there is a social time at breaks.

    - Make connections between group members.

        "Does the problem Sue is having with Philip sound anything like what Mary is talking about? What's alike about them?"

5. **Leading activities**. The group activities provide practice and are a fun part of each session. The instructions are given to you in this *Leader's Guide*, but remember to keep an eye on the time.

6. **Pacing**. It is up to you to keep the group moving through the material. We have included time estimates for each topic, and you may want to put time points throughout the *Leader's Guide* to remind you how fast you are progressing. Although the course is designed for six 2-hour sessions, some groups have chosen to expand to 2 1/2-hour sessions and/or seven to eight sessions.

7. **Generalizing**. Most of the vignettes ring "true-to-life." One or two may seem a little unrealistic. In either case, a single vignette can capture only one of many possible outcomes. The child could have responded differently to the parent's action in every case. To help participants learn to generalize the *Active Parenting Today* skills beyond the vignettes, play "what if" with them.

   > *"What if Janelle doesn't agree to the study time idea? What could Pat do then?"*

8. **Giving feedback**. Each session begins with a Share And Tell period. This provides an opportunity for Home Activities to be shared (building group cohesiveness) and for feedback to help improve skills. In order to be encouraging, you might focus feedback around two areas:

   - *"What did you like about how you handled the situation?"*

   - *"What do you think you could do to improve the way you handled it?"*

9. **Assigning Home Activities**. The program works best when parents complete their Home Activities. Leaders who emphasize the importance of reading the *Parent's Guide* and doing the exercises have a high degree of participation, and their groups run much better.

In Preparation

Before teaching *Active Parenting Today*, it is essential to prepare yourself thoroughly. Consider the following:

1. If you have taken a Leader Certification Workshop, review the materials and notes. Recall the techniques you learned to establish a good learning climate, to generate and encourage participation, and to handle any problems that might occur.

2. Reflect on yourself and your attitude towards the participants. How can you build credibility and positive feelings with them?

3. Make all the advance arrangements—notify the participants if necessary, arrange for the proper facilities, refreshments, equipment, etc. Make sure the environment is as comfortable, bright and conducive to learning as possible.

4. Set up the room for good communication. Make sure you have access to each person, and that each person has a good view of you and your visual aids. We recommend a circle arrangement when possible.

5. Thoroughly study all the materials. Read the study materials, answer the questions and prepare the exercises. Above all, go through the *Leader's Guide* several times. Become completely familiar with it.

6. Rehearse each session. This means actually role-playing or talking yourself through the leader's part. It includes a complete run-through of the appropriate videotapes.

7. Most people find that the hardest part is the first hour—in other words, building the climate with the class. Review the questions in the next section to prepare yourself for creating that climate.

8. Relax! Enjoy it. It's a happy experience. Remember the self-fulfilling prophecy—people tend to behave the way you expect them to behave. Groups tend to go the way you expect them to go.

Interaction Checklist

As you prepare for this seminar, ask yourself the following questions to help you aim the seminar towards the needs of this audience.

Approach

How should I shape my approach—language, vocabulary and examples—considering the group's age, sex, profession, economic level, education, experience or typical way of communication?

Motives

To what degree will I have to help them find reasons and motivation for being here? Are they already eager to come? Or are some of them being forced to come?

Differences

What differences are there in the people coming that might divide the group? How will I acknowledge these differences and make them productive?

Group Dynamics

Are there any intragroup dynamics I should watch for? Are some people shy, are some not? How will I create an atmosphere in which everybody feels free to participate?

A Note on Group Differences

Some groups are outgoing; some are not. The outgoing ones will answer questions freely, volunteer stories, share feelings—in short, participate. The non-outgoing groups will remain silent, not answer questions freely and appear to clam up.

Initially, if you have a silent group, you may think something is wrong with you or your ability to facilitate. But remember this: The so-called silent group is probably just as interested and involved as the outgoing group, but it is just not its style to participate. The participants may be shy, guarded or uncomfortable speaking up in a group.

With these groups, look for head-nodding and note-taking. These behaviors indicate they are interested and are with you. When posing questions, ask them to jot down their responses instead of speaking them. Then ask them to share their answers. You'll be surprised at how freely they will share. All they needed was a little more time to consider and verbalize their answers in private. Remember: The difference between a verbal, outgoing group or individual and a non-verbal, silent group or individual is a difference in style, not a difference in interest.

Tips For Using This Guide

1. Use markers to color-code the various activities (for example, highlight class activities in yellow, video segments in red).

2. The course is designed for 2-hour sessions; however, we have included a lot of material and you may not be able to cover it all in class. Relax. That's one reason participants have the *Parent's Guide*.

3. As you prepare for your session, decide which topics and exercises might be omitted if time is short. Material you may want to share with participants is printed in bold type; the lighter type is meant for you as the group leader. In addition, symbols have been used to key certain aspects of your discussion.

   Indicates a question directed to the group.

   Indicates material you might consider putting on a blackboard or flip chart.

   Indicates the next video segment to show the group.

   Indicates a reference to the *Parent's Guide*, along with the appropriate page numbers.

   Indicates break time for the group.

   Indicates a Notes section.

   Indicates an activity.

   Indicates an optional activity.

4. Most VCRs have a counter, but often the feet indicator is slightly different from one to the other. As you preview the tapes on the VCR you will be using, indicate the footage for each segment in your *Leader's Guide*. This will give you easy access to a segment for review.

5. Protect your tapes by avoiding extreme heat or cold. Keep them in a dry place out of direct sunlight and in the protective program case.

6. Each topic has an estimated amount of time it will take you to cover the material. Next to the time estimate are two blanks: "_____ to _____." This is for you to fill in based on your starting and stopping times for the session. (Use a pencil so that you can change them for your next group if necessary.) For example:

I. Introduction (35 min. <u>7:00</u> to <u>7:35</u>)

The Active Parenting Community

The goal of Active Parenting Publishers is more than just providing you with state-of-the-art parenting education programs. As we grow, we will continue to develop other programs and materials, not only on parenting, but on related topics as well. We would like to meet your needs in providing programs you request.

A second goal of Active Parenting Publishers is to facilitate the networking of parenting educators—in short to put you in touch with each other. *Leader* magazine, as well as our leader training workshops and conferences, are all aimed at achieving this goal.

Please take a few minutes to contribute to our growing network by sharing with us your experiences and successes. We will answer all queries and pass on as many as possible through *Leader* magazine. Thanks!

Parent Evaluation Form

The *Leader's Guide* includes an evaluation form for you to copy and pass out to the parents in your class. This form will provide you with valuable feedback to help you improve as a leader and also to find out what information and exercises parents find most valuable. Please send copies of these evaluations, along with copies of your goal cards, to Active Parenting Publishers so that we can better know the parents who take your classes and be better able to help them.

 Notes _____

_____

_____

_____

_____

_____

_____

_____

_____

_____

_____

_____

_____

_____

_____

_____

_____

_____

_____

_____

_____

_____

_____

_____

_____

_____

_____

_____

Parent Evaluation Form

Active Parenting Today

Please take a moment to help us help you by completing this brief questionnaire. Your answers are important to us, and we thank you for your valuable time.

Name: _____

Address: _____

City: _____ State: _____ Zip: _____

Home Phone: (_____) _____

Work Phone: (_____) _____

About you and your family

❑ Male   ❑ Single   **Highest degree attained:**
❑ Female   ❑ Married   ❑ High School Graduate
    ❑ Divorced   ❑ Undergraduate Degree
         ❑ Graduate Degree

Your race:

❑ African-American   ❑ Hispanic
❑ Asian   ❑ American Indian
❑ Caucasian   ❑ Other

Your age:

❑ 15-20   ❑ 41-50   ❑ 71-80
❑ 21-30   ❑ 51-60   ❑ 80 or above
❑ 31-40   ❑ 61-70

My spouse is also taking *Active Parenting Today* or has already done so.
❑ Yes   ❑ No

What ages are your children? (Check all that apply.)
❑ 0-5   ❑ 6-10   ❑ 11-15   ❑ 16-20   ❑ 21 or older

About your course

Location & Setting:

City _____ State _____

❑ Religious Organization   ❑ School   ❑ Mental Health Center   ❑ Other: _____

Why did you sign up for an Active Parenting course? (Check all that apply.)
- ❏ General desire to improve my parenting skills
- ❏ Help with a specific problem
- ❏ Mandatory attendance (Describe.) _____
- ❏ Other: _____

Please rate the following

Setting:	❏ Excellent	❏ Good	❏ Fair	❏ Poor
Leader:	❏ Excellent	❏ Good	❏ Fair	❏ Poor
Videotapes:	❏ Excellent	❏ Good	❏ Fair	❏ Poor
Parent's Guide:	❏ Excellent	❏ Good	❏ Fair	❏ Poor
Overall experience:	❏ Excellent	❏ Good	❏ Fair	❏ Poor

What were the most helpful aspects of the program? _____

_____

_____

What could be improved? _____

_____

_____

Where did you learn about *Active Parenting Today*? _____

_____

_____

Would you recommend this course/program to a friend? ❏ Yes ❏ No

Are you interested in becoming an *Active Parenting Today* leader? ❏ Yes ❏ No

Check any of the following programs which you might be interested in attending:

- ❏ *Family Talk* : A positive approach to discussing difficult topics with your family.
- ❏ *Windows: Healing and Helping Through Loss:* A sensitive program that guides you through personal loss and examines constructive ways to help others cope with loss.
- ❏ *Active Parenting of Teens:* Active Parenting through your child's tumultuous teen years.
- ❏ *Parents With Careers:* A wealth of knowledge on how to successfully juggle the modern dilemma of career and home life.
- ❏ Other: _____

Optional:
If we may have permission to use these comments to help promote Active Parenting programs, please sign below:

Authorization Signature _____

Success

To laugh often and much; to win the respect of intelligent people and affection of children; to earn the appreciation of honest critics and endure the betrayal of false friends; to appreciate beauty; to find the best in others; to leave the world a bit better, whether by a healthy child, a garden patch or a redeemed social condition; to know even one life has breathed easier because you have lived. This is to have succeeded.

Ralph Waldo Emerson

SESSION **1**

THE ACTIVE PARENT

	Topic	Activity	Video
I	Introductions, Name Tags And Greetings	Icebreaker (optional)	1. Welcome (5:41) 2. All Kinds of Families (2:42) 3. Share And Tell (3:41)
II	What Do We Want For Our Children?	Goal Card (optional)	
III	Styles of Parenting		4. Styles of Parenting, Part 1 (3:58), Part 2 (1:42) and Part 3 (2:48)
IV	Reward And Punishment Often Backfire	Punishment	5. "The Two Peach Rule" (1:32)
V	The Use of Choices	The Method of Choice	6. The Method of Choice (3:07)
VI	Family Enrichment Activity: Taking Time For Fun		7. Family Enrichment Activity: Taking Time For Fun (2:03)
VII	The Buddy System (optional)		
VIII	Video Review		8. Video Review (1:33)
IX	Home Activities		

OBJECTIVES FOR SESSION 1:

- Introduce yourself and members of the group to each other.
- Meet Dr. Popkin and the cast from the video.
- Clarify leader's and participants' roles.
- Develop an understanding of the active style of parenting, and clearly distinguish it from the dictator and doormat styles.
- Understand the use of choices in parenting.
- Begin developing group cohesiveness.

I. Introductions, Name Tags And Greetings (30 min. _____ to _____)

(As parents come in for the first session, have a registration table set up with the following: *Parent's Guide* books, registration list and name tags.)

A. Icebreaker Activity

(Note: This symbol indicates an optional activity throughout this guide.)
(If you plan to do the name tag icebreaker described below, you can use either the *Active Parenting Today* name tags or sheets of construction paper—8 1/2" by 5 1/2." You will also need straight pins and plenty of markers. As you hand participants a name tag and marker, instruct them:)

Please draw a picture of something fun you used to enjoy doing as a child with one or both of your parents, or something fun you enjoy doing with one or more of your children now. Please also put your first name in large letters across the bottom of the picture. This isn't an art test—stick figures are fine!

B. Welcome

(Welcome parents to the *Active Parenting Today* group and introduce yourself.)

Before we begin, there are several general questions participants normally want answered. Let me deal with those questions now.

C. Who Am I?

I'd like to share a little bit about myself and why I'm excited to be here as your group leader.

30

(Explain who you are, your background, and any other relevant information for the participants. If you are a parent, share something about your children. If you are not a parent, share something about your experience with children. This is also a good time to acknowledge and thank any sponsors who have helped make your group possible.)

Notes _____

_____

_____

_____

_____

_____

_____

_____

_____

_____

D. What Is My Role?

Let me explain my role in this course. I'm not here to do a lot of lecturing, although I will share some information with you. My primary job is to facilitate the learning process, introduce the ideas of this program to you, moderate the discussion, clarify some of the concepts whenever I can, and most important, help you apply the information from the video and *Parent's Guide* to your own families.

E. Who Are You?

Let's take a few minutes to go around the group and introduce yourselves. We'll take more time to get to know each other later, so for now I'd like you to share your names, the names and ages of your children and one other fact you'd like to share (■ and the fun picture that you drew on your name tag).
(Keep the group moving. These are brief introductions.)

F. What Is Active Parenting?

To tell you more about the program, I'd like to introduce you to Dr. Michael Popkin, the author of *Active Parenting Today*, and to Kevin Loring, the program's narrator. Let's take a look at our first video.

Welcome

• • • • • • • • • • • • • • • • • • •

 Please turn to the Notes pages at the back of your *Parent's Guide*, and write down one idea from that opening vignette you'd like to take home with you. I'll give you just a minute to jot down one important thought.
(Allow 1 minute.)

Okay, who's willing to share what they wrote down?
(Allow 4 or 5 comments, and limit discussion to under 5 minutes.)

 Active Parenting Today

Why do you think we call this program *"Active" Parenting Today*?
(Listen for answers that reflect "being involved.")

What would be "reactive" parenting?

- Parent <u>rea</u>cts to child's behavior.
- Random discipline.

"Active" Parenting   "Reactive" Parenting

(Encourage each person who shares, then sum up with something like the following:) **In this course we'll be learning ways to be active leaders in our families, rather than just reacting haphazardly to the challenges our children present. Of course, to do this we'll need a solid approach to parenting—along with the information and skills to make it work. That's what this *Active Parenting Today* course is all about.**

Now, let's meet our video families who will help us learn how to take an active approach to parenting.

 Notes _____

_____

_____

_____

_____

_____

All Kinds of Families

 What do you think of these video families, and what the narrator said about learning from families that aren't exactly like ours?
(Encourage responses indicating that "families are more alike than different," that we shouldn't get hung up on whether these families have the same background as ours, or whether they have more or less money than we do.)

G. Ground Rules

 Since we're going to be meeting together for 6 sessions, I think it's important that we agree on some ground rules. First, I'm going to name a few that many groups find helpful. We can add our own as well as modify these:
(Board ground rules and get agreement from the group.)

PG | 10

- Be forgiving of yourself.
  (You might let the group read the section on mistakes on page 10 of the *Parent's Guide*.)

- Be encouraging to each other.

- Be patient.
  (Remind them that this is a 6-session course, and it usually takes 3 or 4 sessions before parents begin to see changes in their children's behavior.)

- Speak as often as you like, but keep your comments brief.
  (This keeps the discussion moving.)

- What is shared in this group stays in this group.
  (Stress confidentiality.)

H. Procedures

Now that we have a better understanding of active parenting, let's talk about how this seminar will be conducted.
(Attempt to establish an atmosphere of learning by emphasizing these:)

- informality
- no testing
- free movement around the room

- participation through questions, discussion and activities
  (No one is forced to participate.)
- buddy system ◣
  (If you plan to use the buddy system described on page 50, let participants know now so they can be thinking about whom to pair up with.)
- survival items (explain locations and/or times of:)
    - restrooms
    - phones
    - breaks
    - starting/stopping times
    - any other housekeeping information
- Parent Completion Certificates ◣
  (If you will be awarding these at the end of your group, this is a good time to show one as an example and to explain any criteria you might have for earning one.)
- Other points:

  _____

  _____

  _____

  _____

  _____

  _____

  _____

I. Share And Tell

An important part of what you'll get out of this program will come from the feedback and encouragement you provide each other. Each week, we will begin our group with what we call Share And Tell. This is a period when you'll discuss how your Home Activities went, and be able to ask for feedback and support from the other group members.

We'll also follow a fourth family as they go through many of the same learning experiences as you. Let's listen to Diane tell us about it.

Notes _____

_____

Share And Tell

 Can any of you relate to what Diane was saying? Where did that hit home? (Allow 2 or 3 comments.)

We saw that Jim stayed home with the kids. I notice in our group we have a number of fathers present (if this is true)**, and I want to compliment them as leaders of a growing trend toward more active participation by men in parenting.**

We'll be following Diane's progress week to week, as we continue our own.

II. What Do We Want For Our Children? (15 min. _____ to _____)

A. The Purpose of Parenting

If we are really going to understand how to do a job well, it's important to know the purpose of that job.

 So, to begin with, what is the purpose of parenting? (Accept all answers.)

> The purpose of parenting:
> To protect and prepare children

Because the world is often dangerous, we must protect children while at the same time preparing them.

 And what are we preparing them to do? (Accept all answers.)

> The purpose of parenting:
> To protect and prepare children
> To survive and thrive

All animals—even humans—seek to survive, but because humans have more potential than other animals, we also have a higher goal, which we call "thriving."

Finally, where is it that we are preparing our children to survive and thrive?
(Prod if they have trouble . . . "Under a dictatorship? In the jungles of South America?")

> The purpose of parenting:
> To protect and prepare children
> To survive and thrive
> In the kind of society in which they live.

And in what kind of society do our children live?

- **Right, a democratic society.**

B. Four Key Qualities

The qualities it takes to survive and thrive in a modern democratic society are different from those it might take to survive and thrive under a dictatorship or in a society with no laws.

Dictator   Democratic   Lawless

Imagine that you were hired to consult with a dictator about the qualities he would want instilled in the children of his country to help them survive. What qualities would you suggest?
(Board under "Dictator" as a list. Example:)

Dictator   Democratic   Lawless
- fearful
- blindly obedient
- no belief in free will

Notes _____

_____

_____

Now let's say you were hired as a consultant for a lawless society—one where there are no laws and no government—like the Wild West in American history. What qualities would enable children to survive in that kind of society?
(Board under "Lawless," using words like these:)

Dictator	Democratic	Lawless
		• strong-willed
		• violent
		• self-centered
		• insensitive to others

 Now imagine that you were hired as a consultant by an elected president of a democracy, and she wanted to know what qualities would enable children not only to survive, but also to thrive. What would be some of the qualities you would list?
(Board under "Democratic." Be sure to bring these out:)

Dictator	Democratic	Lawless
	• responsible	
	• cooperative	
	• high self-esteem	
	• courageous	

All of the qualities you've named are worthwhile and help children to thrive. However, 4 qualities seem to form the foundation for all others:

- **Responsibility -** the ability to make decisions and accept the outcome of those decisions
- **Cooperation -** the ability to work together with others toward a common goal
- **Courage -** confidence to take a known risk for a known purpose
- **Self-esteem -** having a high opinion of yourself, and confidence in your ability to succeed

Notes _____

_____

_____

C. Goal Card Activity

I have some goal cards I'd like to pass out.
(Pass out the goal cards at this time.)

Let's go over these goal cards together. At the top are lines for information I'd like to have for my records—name, address, phone numbers, etc. Under the Purpose of Parenting and the 4 key qualities listed, you'll notice 2 identical boxes and a line in each that starts with "Child's Name."

1. **Write the name of one of your children on one of those lines.**
   (Pause.)

2. **Under that, in the left column of the box, you'll notice a list of the 4 key qualities—responsibility, cooperation, courage, self-esteem. Next to each is a scale from 1 to 10. Thinking about the child you've named at the top, how would you rate him on the first quality —responsibility—at this time? If you think he handles responsibility well, you might put a dot under the number 8, 9 or 10. If you think your child needs some work in that area, you might put a dot under 1, 2, 3 or 4.**

3. **Now consider your child's ability to cooperate with others, and rate her on this characteristic from 1 (needs work) to a 10 (high level). Put a dot under one of the numbers next to the word "cooperation. " Follow the same procedure with the other 2 key qualities—courage and self-esteem.**

4. **After you've finished that step, you'll notice there are 4 lines under the word "self-esteem" where you can add other key qualities you would like to see your child develop. For example, if you would like her to develop the quality of honesty, write the word "honesty" on one of the lines. Then, rate how you think your child demonstrates that quality.**

5. **Let's look back over the scale to see where you've placed the dots. Where you've put dots in the 6-to-10 range are the areas where you think your child's strengths lie. 1s, 2s or 3s are areas where you think your child needs some work. Wherever there are problem areas, there are opportunities for improvement.**

6. Turning over the card, let's look under the next section called "Opportunities/Goals." There is room for you to write down 3 problems for each child. For example, if I had rated my child's sense of responsibility as "2," I might write here a specific time when he demonstrates poor handling of responsibility, such as, "He forgets to give me the notes he brings home from school."

7. On the next line, we can change the problem into an opportunity by writing in what you want to happen. "I want Stephen to remember to give me the school notes." Now, fill in at least one of these problems that you would like to address in this course and at least one opportunity.

8. Complete the same information for each child in your family. If you have more than 2 children, let me know and I'll give you additional cards. If you are here with a spouse, I suggest you work on separate cards and then compare. Are there any questions about how these goal cards work?
(Clarify any questions or misunderstandings.)

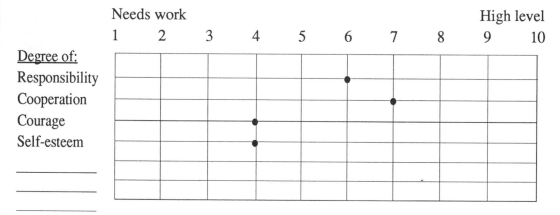

(Note: The goal cards serve as both a way to focus your parents' attention on the goals and purposes of the program and as a pre-test/post-test measure for you to use in quantifying the success of your course. For this reason, we suggest that parents turn in their goal cards and you keep them throughout the program. This will prevent them from being misplaced, and prevent children from inadvertently seeing their parents' ratings.)
(Allow 3 or 4 minutes.)

Let's stop now and do a bit of sharing. As we go around the group, I'd like each of you to share briefly one of the Opportunities/Goals that you'll be working on with each of your children.

(Move around the circle, allowing each person to share. To save time, have each person share in small groups of 3 to 4.)

Notes _____

_____

_____

Break (10 min. _____ to _____)

III. Styles of Parenting (20 min. _____ to _____)

We've talked about some of the qualities we want our children to have, and some of the problem areas that become opportunities for instilling these qualities. How do we as parents achieve these goals? This next video is about 3 different styles of parenting that people use.

[# 4] Styles of Parenting, Part 1

• •

 What style of parenting is this? Dictator? Doormat? Or active parent?

　　● dictator

	Dictator	Doormat	Active Parent
Who makes the rules?			
Why?			
How are rules enforced?			

40

Who makes the rules under the dictator style of parenting?

- the parent
  (Add the word "parent" to the chart under Dictator.)

 And when the child asks *why,* what does Dad say?

- "Because I'm the parent and I said so."
  (Add that quote to the chart.)

Under a dictatorship, whether it's a king or queen or parent, how are rules enforced?

- reward and punishment
  (Add that to the chart.)

Did Dad's dictator style of parenting seem to work?

- No, it just produced a power struggle.

Let's continue with the video and see another style of parenting.

 ## Styles of Parenting, Part 2

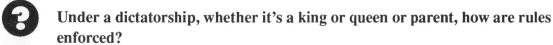

What style of parenting is Janelle's mother using in this vignette?

- doormat

 Who makes the rules with the doormat style of parenting?

- the child
  (Add to the chart.)

 Why? What do Mother's actions seem to say?

- "Because you're the child and you say so."
  (Add to the chart.)

 And how are the rules enforced in this style of parenting?

- They aren't.
  (Add to the chart.)

Did Mother's doormat style of parenting seem to work?

- No. Janelle is not learning responsibility or cooperation.

Let's watch the video and see how the active style of parenting differs from the dictator and doormat styles—how Mother can be an active parent.

 ## Styles of Parenting, Part 3

 After watching that video, who makes the rules in the active style of parenting?

- the parent, with the child's input, or the parent and child together

 Why is the rule made?

- "Because the situation calls for it."
  (Add to the chart.)

 What did Dad say this time about why the room should be kept neat?

- "Because in our family we take pride in our home, and that means keeping things reasonably neat."

This is a much more powerful thing to say—not "because *I* said so," but "because *the situation* says so."

 And how are rules enforced in an active style of parenting?
(Board answers since they will not know these terms yet.)

- natural and logical consequences
- "I" messages
- problem solving
- encouragement

 Notes _____

_____

_____

_____

_____

	Dictator	**Doormat**	**Active Parent**
Who makes the rules?	Parent	Child	Parent and Child
Why?	Parent says so.	Child says so.	Situation calls for it.
How are rules enforced?	Reward and Punishment	They aren't.	Natural and logical consequences; "I" messages; problem solving; encouragement.

We'll be learning about these and other methods in this program.

What other differences did you notice with the active style of parenting?

- Parents were respectful of Janelle, and they expected her to be respectful of them.

This concept of "mutual respect" is essential in democratic living.

- They discussed the problem with her beforehand.

The child's right to participate—to share what she thinks or feels—is also an essential part of active parenting, just as it is in life in a democratic society. In fact, in *Active Parenting Today* we like to say that "democracy doesn't mean you always get your way; it means you always get your say."

The parent is still the leader and authority in the family—but leads with mutual respect and encourages participation by the child.

IV. Reward And Punishment Often Backfire (10 min. _____ to _____)

A. Reward Becomes a Right

The problem with using rewards to get a child to do what a situation calls for is that the reward very soon becomes a right. In other words, the child expects a reward every time he does what you want him to do.

43

For example, a mother in an *Active Parenting Today* group shared how she wanted her child to "behave" in a grocery store. She finally promised him a toy racing car if he would just be quiet for her to do the shopping. He was quiet and she gave him the car. "However," she said, "I paid dearly for that because every time we went back to the grocery store he wanted another prize for behaving."

Can you think of times when you've used rewards and found that they led to this kind of "what's in it for me?" attitude?
(Allow 2 or 3 examples.)

Later in the program, we'll see how encouragement and logical consequences can be used in place of rewards to build on the positive. Now, I'll give you an idea of how punishment often backfires in a democratic society. Let's do an activity.

B. Punishment Activity

I'd like each of you to find a partner.

Decide which one of you will play the parent and which the child. Okay, parents stand up, and children, get on your knees right up against them. That's it, get short!

There are a lot of ways to dish out punishment, but we're only going to use gestures and verbal ones in this activity.

1. Here's the first situation: Your child has taken a marker and is using the kitchen wall as a coloring book. Okay, parents, now really scold your child; be sure to insult and threaten him . . . and get out your pointing finger.
(Allow about 20-30 seconds of scolding.)

2. Okay, this time punish your child for not doing her homework.
(Allow 20-30 seconds again.)

3. This time you'll be punishing him for ignoring your requests to set the table. Okay, really go to it!
(Allow 20-30 seconds.)

Now, it's time for turn-about's-fair-play. Parents become the children and vice versa. That's it, change positions.

1. Okay, new parents, I want you to punish your child for hitting her little sister. Never mind that by spanking her you taught her hitting was the way to solve problems. Go ahead and really scold her.
   (Allow 20-30 seconds.)

All right, let's regroup and discuss what we learned.

What was the experience like for you?
(Encourage sharing, emphasizing such points as these:)

- I felt small and helpless.
- I felt defiant.
- I felt treated unfairly.
- I felt foolish treating another adult this way.

Did any of you who were children the first go-round feel like getting even?

Or that it was "only fair" when you got a chance to punish back?

Or even that it was unfair because you only got to punish once and they had 3 turns?
(Allow 2-3 comments.)

What's the point here? In a society of equals, when you punish someone who considers herself your equal, you give her the right to ... what?

- punish you back

Have you ever experienced this retaliation with a child of yours ... or did you ever punish your parents back?
(Allow comments.)

Well, if punishment doesn't work well with today's children, why do we keep doing it? In fact, why do we continue to use the dictator and doormat styles of parenting at all?
(Allow brief discussion, leading to the next video.)

Let's see how this next video makes some of the same points you've been making. In later sessions we'll be seeing some ways to handle these examples we've role-played using active parenting methods.

 ## "The Two Peach Rule"

What's the point of this story?

- When a rule becomes tradition, it is continued just because "that's the way it's always been done."

Where did our parenting traditions come from? What continent?

- Europe

And back in that society in Europe, based on a hierarchy where everyone "knew his place," what were the "rules" or methods of parenting that were effective?

- reward and punishment

So, in a democratic society we find that it's time to change our ways of parenting to other techniques of discipline and encouragement that will be more effective. And that's what we'll be doing in this seminar.

 Notes _____

_____

_____

V. The Use of Choices (15 min. _____ to _____)

A. The Method of Choice

We're now going to talk about one of the most important concepts in the human experience. This concept is so important—so powerful—that wars have been fought over it. The concept, in a word, is "choice."

 Choice

? **Any ideas about why this is such a powerful concept?**
(Allow a brief discussion. You might mention Webster's definition of choice as "the right or privilege of choosing," and the definition of choosing, "to select those most desirable; take by preference." It seems it is just human nature to want to select our own preference.)

Let's take a look at a video that suggests how this powerful concept comes into play in parenting.

The Method of Choice

? **Are there any comments or questions about this video segment?**
(Discuss as needed.)

Dictator	Doormat	Active/Democratic

Remember, we talked about the dictator style of parenting as allowing very tight limits with no freedom.

? **What freedom are we talking about?**

- freedom of choice

? **In the vignette we just saw, what happened when Mother used this dictator approach to try to get Zack to put on his shirt?**

- He refused—rebelled.

We also talked about the doormat approach, where the parent allows too much freedom of choice.

? **What could Zack have worn if his mother were taking this doormat approach?**

- anything he wanted to

And how about the active style of parenting? How does choice fit in here?

- freedom of choice, with limits on those choices

 And what happened when Mother allowed Zack some freedom to choose—when she offered him a choice between two shirts?

- They were able to find a mutually acceptable alternative to the white shirt.

This is an important point. When we start thinking in terms of choice, we begin to move from power struggles with our children to problem solving with them. Finding alternatives that are acceptable to both parent and child is a way out of the hassles. It's also a way to begin preparing children to become good decision makers—that's particularly important when they become teenagers and face such life-threatening choices as those about drugs and sex.

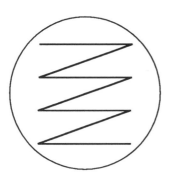

The key is to give simple choices with tighter limits to young children, then gradually expand the amount of freedom as the child gets older. For example, with 7-year-old Sara, Mrs. Mendoza could give the choice of having broccoli or peas. But with 10-year-old Janelle, the limits could be expanded so that Mrs. Matthews would ask her daughter to actually help in planning the weekly menu. You want to balance your choices with the child's age and level of responsibility.

B. The Method of Choice Activity

I'd like you to get into groups of 4 or 5 and brainstorm some of the choices you can begin working on with your children this week at home. The choices might be in any number of areas, for example, dressing, eating, playing or even working. Talk about the kinds of choices you have used in the past, places where you haven't given choices but could, and generally just help each other think about how to expand your use of this very powerful concept. If you'll look in

PG | 24 your *Parent's Guide* on page 24, there's a place to jot down a specific choice you can give each child this week at home. During your discussion, please try to fill in at least 1 example of the new type of choice you can work on.
(Allow 5 minutes.)

? Before we move on, would anyone share what you've learned from this section?
(Allow 2 or 3 comments, as time allows.)

PG | 24 Experiment with giving choices at home this week, and be sure to fill in page 24 in your *Parent's Guide* so we can talk about your experiences next week during Share And Tell.

VI. Family Enrichment Activity: Taking Time For Fun
(5 min. _____ to _____)

The most important part of this course is what you do between sessions.

I'd like you to see another video segment now, what we call our Family Enrichment Activity. Dr. Popkin will go over this with you on the video, suggesting something for you to practice at home each week. Then, at the beginning of each session I'll ask some of you to share how you completed your Family Enrichment Activity and what you experienced.

[#7] Family Enrichment Activity: Taking Time For Fun

PG | 21 I'd like you to turn in your *Parent's Guide* to page 21 so we can review some of the tips for your Family Enrichment Activity.
(Briefly go over the tips in the *Parent's Guide*.)

PG | 21 If you'll also notice on page 23 of your *Parent's Guide*, there is a chart for you to fill in what you do at home this week with your children. Next week we'll share our experiences.

Notes _____

_____

_____

VII. The Buddy System (6 min. _____ to _____)

I mentioned earlier that you'd be choosing a buddy at the end of the session. Let me tell you a little about this "buddy system," as we call it. The idea of support and encouragement is not only important for helping children learn, it's also important for us adults as well. For this reason we'd like you to choose a buddy (there's that concept "choice") to work with over these 6 weeks. The idea is to make one telephone call to each other at some time during the week. This call has 3 purposes:

Buddy System

1. Discuss the reading from the *Parent's Guide*.
2. See how the home assignments are going, and offer encouragement.
3. Talk about applying the concepts that have been covered to situations with your children.

Are there any questions about the buddy system?
(Answer questions and modify the system to meet your needs.)

Okay, please find a buddy to pair up with.
(We recommend that couples not buddy up with each other. If you have an odd number of participants, you can either have one group of 3 or be a buddy yourself. After buddies are chosen, continue.)

Okay, let's take 2 minutes for you to talk with your buddy a little bit about the types of activities you and your child might choose for this week's Family Enrichment Activity. Just get to know each other a bit, and brainstorm some choices.

VIII. Video Review (2 min. _____ to _____)

Before we conclude each session, I'd like you to see a quick video review of the key concepts and information from the session. Let's watch.

Notes _____

_____

_____

_____

IX. Home Activities (2 min. _____ to _____)

(Note: Please emphasize the importance of the Home Activities, and get agreement. This will improve the quality of your future sessions tremendously, as well as how much the parents get out of the course.)

 Before we leave, please turn to page 25 in your *Parent's Guide* and take a look at the Home Activities. I can't emphasize enough the importance this week of doing the activities listed here:

HOME ACTIVITIES

1. Read Chapter 1 in your *Parent's Guide*.
   If you wish to read ahead, please do so.
2. Do the Family Enrichment Activity: Taking Time For Fun on page 23.
3. Practice giving choices to your children this week and complete the Method of Choice Activity Sheet on page 24.
4. Call your buddy (optional).

Will everyone make time to do these this week?
(Try to get everyone nodding their heads in the affirmative.)

Great! Be sure to check them off in your *Parent's Guide* as you do them. See you next week! And remember, "Every day a little play."

Notes _____

_____

_____

_____

_____

	Topic	Activity	Video
I	Share And Tell		1. Share And Tell (2:42)
II	Courage And Self-Esteem		2. "Courage And Fear" (1:10) 3. Think-Feel-Do Cycle, Part 1 (7:06) and Part 2 (1:28)
III	Turning Discouragement Into Encouragement	Encouragement Video Practice	4. Encouragement Video Practice 1 (2:18), Practice 2 (3:07), Practice 3 (1:23), Practice 4 (2:23) and Practice 4 continued (:58)
IV	Encouragement Activities	Building on Strengths Encouragement Circle	
V	Family Enrichment Activity: Letter of Encouragement		5. Family Enrichment Activity: Letter of Encouragement (2:08)
VI	Video Review		6. Video Review (1:00)
VII	Home Activities		

OBJECTIVES FOR SESSION 2:

• •

- Understand the relationship between thinking, feeling and doing.
- Understand the relationship between self-esteem, courage, and positive and negative behavior.
- Identify 4 ways parents discourage their children.
- Identify 4 ways parents can encourage their children.
- Practice building encouragement skills.

I. Share And Tell (15 min. _____ to _____)

(As parents come back for the second session, you can either have the name tags on the table for them to pick up, or pass them out after parents are all seated. ◢ We suggest you pass out the goal cards after parents are seated, which gives you a way to check attendance at the same time. Be sure to collect both at the end of the session.)

Welcome back. We've got an exciting session planned. Let's begin by checking in on our video Share And Tell family, the Davidsons. If you remember from last week, Diane was in a power struggle with her daughter Stephanie. Let's see if she was able to make any progress with her Family Enrichment Activity and other assignments.

Share And Tell

• •

Any thoughts or comments about that vignette?
(Allow 2 or 3 comments.)

Even though things are not much different for Diane, do you get a sense that she is at least a little hopeful?
(Try to bring up the idea that things won't change overnight, but they will improve over time.)

Let's talk a little about last week's Family Enrichment Activity, which was "Taking Time For Fun." Please turn in your *Parent's Guide* to page 23. How many of you completed the guide sheet for Taking Time For Fun?
(Acknowledge those who did, and encourage everyone to fill out these pages at home each week.)

? **I find it helpful to begin with successes, so with that in mind, who had a success this week in taking time to have fun with their children?**
(Allow 2 or 3 to share their experiences. You might encourage clapping, if you like, for having the courage to share.)

? **Did anyone run into a problem with the Family Enrichment Activity that they'd like the group's feedback on?**
(Allow 2 or 3, if any, to share, and encourage the group to give feedback and make positive suggestions.)

 We also had as a home assignment this week to practice giving your children choices. Please turn in your *Parent's Guide* to page 24 for that activity.

? **How many of you completed this page?**
(Again, acknowledge those who did, and encourage all to follow through with the home portion of the course.)

? **Who had a success with the use of choices that they would be willing to share?**
(Allow 2 or 3 to share their experiences, and continue to offer encouragement.)

? **Did anyone run into a problem with this activity?**
(Again, allow 2 or 3, if any, to share, and encourage feedback and positive suggestions.)

? **You also had as a home assignment to read Chapter 1 in your *Parent's Guide*. How many of you followed through with that assignment?**
(Stress importance of doing the reading.)

◩ **Finally, we had one other home assignment. Do you remember what it was?**

- to call your buddy

? **How many of you talked to your buddy over the week?**

? **How did it go? What was the experience like for you?**
(Allow 2 or 3 people to share, encouraging the group to stick with it and support each other in this way.)

II. Courage And Self-Esteem (30 min. _____ to_____)

A. Courage

During the first session, we said we'd be focusing on instilling **4 particular qualities in our children that would improve their chances of surviving and thriving in a democratic society. Who remembers what those 4 qualities were?**

- courage
- self-esteem
- responsibility
- cooperation

Today, we're going to be looking at the first 2, and in many ways the most basic of those qualities, courage and self-esteem. So to begin, what is courage?
(Accept all answers.)

All of your ideas make sense, but just so we can use a common definition, let's say this:

Courage is the confidence to take a known risk for a known purpose.

Using this as our definition, why do you suppose courage is so important? While you're thinking about that question, let's watch the second video, which portrays the poem "Courage and Fear" by Dr. Popkin. As you listen to the words of that poem, think about your own childhood and the times you've had to face your own fears.

Notes _____

_____

_____

_____

_____

_____

_____

_____

_____

"Courage And Fear"

 Can any of you remember a time in your childhood when courage and fear had a similar battle?
(Allow 2 or 3 to share if they are willing.)

Let me ask that earlier question again. Why is courage such an important quality to instill in our children?

- So they won't live a life filled with regret for having missed out on the many opportunities and experiences life has to offer.

If courage is the confidence to take a known risk, it is crucial to our lives because there is no other quality you can develop that doesn't require some risk. For example, to become responsible you have to risk the consequences of your choices.

What are some other examples of when a child might need courage?
(Accept all examples.)

- courage to stick with a difficult task in school
- courage to try new skills when failure might be embarrassing
- courage to resist peer pressure

When in your children's lives will the courage to resist peer pressure become crucial?

- in the preteen and teen years when they are offered drugs

By the way, does anyone know where the word "courage" itself comes from?

"coeur"

It comes from the French word "coeur," meaning heart. Courage is the heart of human potential. It is the feeling of confidence we have in ourselves that says there is a reasonable chance we can succeed if we take that risk.

B. Self-Esteem

What do you think it takes for people to have the confidence to take a known risk for a known purpose, in other words, to have courage?

- They have to think they are capable of succeeding. They have to have what we call "high self-esteem."

You may have noticed that we are talking about two slightly different things: how we *think* about ourselves—self-esteem—and how we *feel* about ourselves— encouraged or discouraged. Let's look at a video that helps us understand a little better how the thinking and feeling aspects affect our behavior.

C. Think-Feel-Do Cycle

Think-Feel-Do Cycle, Part 1

Did anyone identify with Sara in that last scene? How did you feel watching her? (Be sure to emphasize feeling words in their responses, for example, "afraid," "angry," "hurt.")

What was Dad trying to accomplish by saying what he did?

- to motivate her to cross the log

Dad obviously wasn't successful. Although he tried to encourage Sara, his words were actually very discouraging. Why was that?

- Telling her not to be a baby was a put-down.
- He actually lowered her self-esteem, thereby lowering her courage.

Now, let's go back to the same situation and see how Dad could be more encouraging.

 # 3 *Think-Feel-Do Cycle, Part 2*

● ●

 How do you feel this time?
(Emphasize feeling words again, for example, "encouraged," "great," "proud," "satisfied.")

How was Dad more encouraging this time?

- He reminded her of past successes on the balance beam.
- He found a half-way point that was more equal to the amount of courage she had.
- He used a lot of verbal encouragement: "attagirl," "you're doing great."
- He didn't get frustrated or angry.

Break (10 min. _____ to _____)

III. Turning Discouragement Into Encouragement
(40 min. _____ to _____)

A. Instilling Heart

 **Dis-**

In every situation with our children, we have equal opportunity to dis-courage them—to remove heart . . .

 **En-**

. . . or to en-courage them—to instill heart.

Half of learning how to be more effective encouragers is to first catch ourselves when we are discouraging our children, then avoid doing so.

59

Dis-

Notes _____

_____

_____

_____

B. Encouragement Video Practice

PG | 47

If you'll turn in your *Parent's Guide* to page 47, you'll see a chart that lists 4 vignettes and blocks to fill in what you might think, feel and do if you were the child in each of these situations. In each case I'll pause the tape and let you fill in the blocks. The key is to put yourself in the child's shoes, and see if you can notice what you'd be thinking, feeling and doing. We'll also see if we can identify which of the 4 discouraging influences the parent is using. Let's watch the first one.

 (#4)   **Encouragement Video Practice 1**

● ●

PG | 47

Write down in your *Parent's Guide* what you would be thinking and feeling if you were in Ben's shoes, and what you think your future behavior probably would be. Also, mark discouraging influences in this space.
(Allow about 1 minute.)

? If you were Ben right now, what would you be thinking?
(Encourage sharing.)

? How would you feel?
(Allow sharing.)

60

? **What do you think you might do in the future?**
(Allow sharing.)

? **While we're on the topic of behavior, how cooperative do you think you'd be towards Mother the rest of the day? For that matter, how would you like to be Ben's teacher, if Ben were going to preschool?**
(Allow sharing.)

? **Finally, what were the discouraging influences Mother was using?**

- Negative expectations—"You're too little. You'll spill it."
- Focusing on mistakes—She only comments on the spill, not on the successful walk over to the table.
- Overprotection—She wants to do for Ben what he could learn to do for himself.

Let's take a look at Ben's thinking and then see how Laura could be more encouraging. When we watch the vignette between Laura and Ben, again put yourself in Ben's shoes.

 Encouragement Video Practice 2

● ●

 Please write in your *Parent's Guide* what you would think, feel and do if you were Ben *this time*. Also indicate the encouraging influences that are operating.
(Allow 1 minute.)

? **What would you be thinking this time if you were Ben?**
(Allow sharing.)

? **What would you be feeling?**
(Allow sharing.)

? **And what do you think you would do in the future?**
(Bring out responses that suggest you would continue to try new things, work on your cereal carrying, and probably be more cooperative with Mother.)

Now, let's take a look at the 4 encouraging influences that were described in the video.

 Encouraging influences

- Building on strengths
- Showing confidence
- Showing acceptance/reasonable expectations
- Fostering independence

 Which of these encouraging influences did Mother use to encourage Ben?

- Fostering independence—She let him do it for himself; she let him clean it up.
- Building on strengths—He did a great job walking it over.

 Let's see how this came across to Ben.

Notes _____

_____

_____

_____

_____

 #4 ## Encouragement Video Practice 3

●●

 PG 47 **Once again, write in your *Parent's Guide* what you would think, feel and do if you were Janelle.**
(Allow 1 minute.)

 What would you be thinking if you were Janelle?
(Allow sharing.)

 How would you feel?
(Allow sharing.)

 What do you think you would do in the future?
(Allow sharing.)

? **Which of the discouraging influences was Mother using?**

- Focusing on mistakes—She made no comments about what was done well.
- Perfectionism—"I don't know about this word . . . 'green' is kind of weak."
- Overprotection—Mother is doing Janelle's homework with her.

Now let's see how it came across to Janelle.

 Encouragement Video Practice 4

● ●

 Okay, write in your *Parent's Guide* what you would think, feel and do this time, and list encouraging influences Mother was using.
(Allow 1 minute.)

? **What would you be thinking this time?**
(Allow sharing.)

? **And how would you feel?**
(Allow sharing.)

? **What do you think your future behavior would be—what would you do?**
(Allow sharing.)

? **Which encouraging influences did Pat use with her daughter?**

- Building on strengths—"I especially liked the way you described the boat."
- Showing acceptance—"You're already good enough . . . I'm really glad you're my daughter."
- Stimulating independence—Pat allows Janelle to do homework on her own, providing

  - a quiet place
  - a good light
  - help if she needs it
  - encouragement

Let's go back to the video and take a look inside Janelle's mind.

Separate the deed from the doer.

Thinking about that last bit of video, what do you think this phrase means?

- Although we may take issue and set limits on our children's behavior, we want to avoid shaming a child or attacking a child's personality. Instead we want to show acceptance of her as a person.

    - For example, not "You're such a slob," but instead, "You've made a big mess in here."
    - For example, not "You're such a bad girl," but instead, "That wasn't a very nice thing to do."

Notes _____

_____

_____

_____

_____

_____

_____

IV. Encouragement Activities (15 min. _____ to _____)

A. Building on Strengths Activity

Like any other skill, encouragement skills improve with practice. We're now going to have a chance to practice a little encouragement.

PG | 48

Please turn in your *Parent's Guide* to page 48, entitled "Building on Strengths Activity." I'll give you 3 minutes to fill out the page, thinking about yourself and your family.
(Allow 3 minutes or so.)

✳ **B. Encouragement Circle Activity**

I'd like you to pair up (◢ with your buddy) and get with another pair so that we have groups of 4.

(3 is okay; 5 takes too long to complete the activity.)

 | PG | 48 | **Is everyone in a group? Great. We'll call them "encouragement circles." The first part of this activity is to share the strengths that you wrote on page 48 of your *Parent's Guide*. Each person should share a line, then go to the next person. Continue sharing as you go around the circle until I stop you. And don't be afraid to toot your own horn, since encouragement begins at home.**

? **Are there any questions?** (Clarify.) **Okay, do some bragging about yourself and your family!**
(Wait 3-4 minutes.)

Since we've been dealing with methods to help you encourage your children, and since that may not always be easy for you, it is fitting that we give you a little encouragement—or better, that *you* give you a little encouragement.

En-

"One thing I like about you is_____."

- Be direct.
- Be specific.
- Be sincere.
- Say, "Thank you."

Now you'll have an opportunity to practice encouraging each other and to experience the benefits of encouragement directly. Everyone will take a turn as the one encouraged. All the other group members will share something they like about that person. Begin by saying, "One thing I like about you is . . ." When each person in the group has encouraged that person, begin encouraging the next person.

The "rules" of this activity are:

- Speak directly to the person when encouraging him or her.
- Be as specific as possible. For example, say, "I like how patient you are when you listen to other people," as opposed to saying, "You're a nice person."
- Be sincere. If you don't know the person very well, it's okay to be superficial (e.g., "I like your smile . . . your eyes . . . the outfit you are wearing . . .")
- When being encouraged, accept it. Don't put yourself down with such phrases as "No, I'm not really like that," or "You wouldn't say that if you really knew me." Say, "Thank you."

(Answer any questions they might have. Allow 5 to 7 minutes.)

Let's discuss this a little bit.

How do you feel? Anyone feel good?

Why do you think you feel better now than when we began this activity?

How do you feel about the others in your group? Cooperative?

Would you be willing to work on a problem with them if one came up?

What is the lesson in this for our families?

- When we encourage each other—focus on strengths instead of weaknesses—we feel better and are willing to be more cooperative when problems come up.

Notes _____

_____

_____

_____

_____

_____

_____

V. Family Enrichment Activity: Letter of Encouragement (5 min. _____ to _____)

It's now time for our Family Enrichment Activity. I think you'll find it very . . . encouraging.

 Family Enrichment Activity: Letter of Encouragement

 Are there any questions about how to write your letter? You'll find the tips that Dr. Popkin mentioned on page 44 of your *Parent's Guide*.

 (Answer questions, and if there is time, let them work on a draft of their letters and share.)

Please be sure to give a letter to each of your children this week. And be aware that if there has been a lot of stress between you, your child may react negatively to the letter. Don't let that discourage you. Your words can have a positive impact anyway.

Notes _____

_____

_____

_____

_____

_____

_____

_____

_____

_____

_____

_____

_____

_____

_____

VI. Video Review (2 min. ____ to ____)

Let's review what we have covered this session by watching the video review.

◖ #6 ◗ Video Review

• • • • • • • • • • • • • • • • • •

VII. Home Activities (2 min. ____ to ____)

 Your Home Activities for this week are listed on **page 51** of your *Parent's Guide.* I'll read the list aloud.

HOME ACTIVITIES

1. **Read Chapter 2 in your *Parent's Guide.* If you wish to read ahead, please do so.**
2. **Write each child a letter of encouragement, completing page 46.**
3. **Concentrate on making encouraging statements this week, and record your progress on the chart on page 49.**
4. **Complete the Stimulating Independence Activity on page 50.**
5. **Continue "every day a little play" and giving choices from Chapter 1.**
6. **Call your buddy (optional).**

Please leave your name tags and goal cards on the table. And have a great week. I'll see you next _____.

Notes _____

_____

_____

_____

_____

Notes

SESSION 3

UNDERSTANDING YOUR CHILD

	Topic	Activity	Video
I	**Share And Tell**		1. Share And Tell (2:20)
II	**Understanding Behavior**	Two-Hand Push Four Goals Video Practice	2. Goals of Behavior Part 1 (2:50) and Part 2 (4:15) 3. Active Style Revisited (1:33) Four Goals Video Practice: 4. Zack - Negative (1:42) 5. Zack - Active (1:29) 6. Jade - Negative (1:08) 7. Jade - Active (1:35) 8. Ramon - Negative (1:06) 9. Ramon - Active (:45)
III	**Four Goals at Home**	Analyzing The Problem	
IV	**Family Enrichment Activity: Teaching Skills**		10. Family Enrichment Activity: Teaching Skills (2:13)
V	**Video Review**		11. Video Review (1:08)
VI	**Home Activities**		

OBJECTIVES FOR SESSION 3:

- Recognize 4 goals of behavior and their discouraged approaches.
- Recognize how parents influence their children and vice versa.
- Identify how parents sometimes "pay off" misbehavior.
- Each parent will analyze the misbehavior of one of his or her children by identifying the goal and mistaken approach.

(Note: The theoretical nature of this session may challenge some parents. Don't be concerned if they do not grasp the content completely. They will be able to build on their exposure to these concepts as they focus on the concrete skills modeled then taught in later sessions.)

I. Share And Tell (15 min. ____ to ____)

Welcome to our third session of *Active Parenting Today*, "Understanding Your Child." Those of you who like to understand why things are the way they are will really enjoy this session. And those of you who like to learn new skills first are going to see examples of the methods we will be learning in the remaining sessions.)

To begin our Share And Tell for this week, let's hear how things went for Diane in her group.

 Share And Tell

 Can any of you relate to Diane?
(Allow sharing.)

Diane was expecting to see improvement too fast. Remember, we're just beginning to learn this approach to parenting. There are a lot of skills she needs to handle, like the unexpected "none of the above" type answers kids can give.

What mistake did she make with her encouragement skills?

- She tried to use them to manipulate Stephanie, so she didn't sound sincere.

How did it go with your own attempts at encouragement? Who has a success to share about your letter of encouragement?
(Share and discuss.)

Were there any problems with your letters?

Finally, did you continue taking time for fun?

II. Understanding Behavior

(70 min. _____ to _____; 35 min. to break; 35 min. following break)

(Brief b/c tape self-explanatory)

A. Think-Feel-Do Review

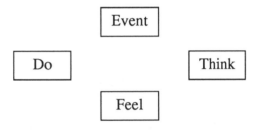

We talked last session about the relationship among 3 very important functions: thinking, feeling and doing.

Would someone tell me the relationship among these 3 functions and the events that happen to us in our lives?
(Add the arrows as someone tells you where they go.)

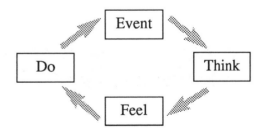

- The events in our lives trigger our thinking about those events—not *cause* our thinking, but *trigger*.
- Our thinking about the event causes our feelings.
- Our thinking and feelings cause our behavior.
- Our behavior influences the event *and* our thinking.

(Be sure to encourage the person who has shared.)

? **Let's review a little more. Where in this model is self-esteem located?**

- In Think. Self-esteem is our thinking about ourselves and our value and worth.

? **And what important *feeling* does self-esteem influence?**

- Courage

Right. When our self-esteem is high, we have *confidence* in our ability to succeed. So we behave in positive ways.

? **But what about when our self-esteem is low? What happens?**

- We become *discouraged* and are more likely to misbehave.

B. Goals, Not Causes

Positive behavior and negative behavior are the real topics for this session. And our goal is to learn how to better influence our children away from negative behavior and towards positive behavior.

Cause $\longrightarrow$ Behavior $\longrightarrow$ Goal

As you watch this next video, look for the answer to a very important question about behavior: Is behavior determined by *causes* in the past, or by our goals for the future? Let's watch.

 ## Goals of Behavior, Part 1

● ●

? **How many of you identified with Dad and found yourself getting angry at Janelle, too?**

? **It's pretty easy for our kids to hook our anger, isn't it?**

Unfortunately, when we get angry, we usually just make matters worse. To understand why, we need to consider 3 things:

- the child's *behavior*—in this case, refusing to clean up when asked
- the child's goals—what she *really* wanted
- and how the parent *pays off* the misbehavior

We are about to see how 4 key goals underlie most of children's negative behavior, and how parents often pay off this misbehavior.

 ## Goals of Behavior, Part 2

• •

 Are there any questions or comments about the 4 goals?
(Answer briefly, postponing any questions that will be covered in the next section.)

I think what is really important about the concept of the 4 goals is to recognize that children can approach them from either of two directions: positive behavior or negative behavior. Let's explore this a little further.

Negative Behavior	Child's Goals	Positive Behavior
	Contact Power Protection Withdrawal	

 Let's think about children for a minute.

Notes _____

_____

_____

_____

_____

_____

_____

_____

? **What are some positive ways they have of achieving the goal of contact?**

- helping us
- playing with others
- getting recognized for successes

? **Thank you. Now, what are some negative ways that children sometimes achieve their goal of contact, using what we call "undue attention-seeking"?**

- being forgetful
- acting helpless
- being lazy

Negative Behavior	Child's Goals	Positive Behavior
Undue attention-seeking	Contact Power Protection Withdrawal	Contributing, cooperating

(Allow 2 or 3 examples of undue attention-seeking. Continue to ask for examples of positive and negative approaches to each goal, building the following chart:)

Negative Behavior	Child's Goals	Positive Behavior
Undue attention-seeking	Contact	Contributing, cooperating
Rebellion	Power	Independence
Revenge	Protection	Assertiveness, forgiveness
Avoidance	Withdrawal	Time alone

C. How To Determine a Child's Goals

? **Why do you think children sometimes take the negative approach to achieving their goals? Why don't they always just choose positive behavior?**

- The negative approach is sometimes the easier aproach.
- The parents often pay off the negative approach.

? So, if we want to avoid paying off misbehavior—the negative approach to the goal—it would help if we could determine what the child's goal is. For example, how can you know if your child is pursuing the goal of contact through the negative approach of undue attention-seeking?

There are two clues:

1. How we feel. We find that different negative approaches and goals bring about different feelings in parents.

2. How the child responds to correction. In other words, what he does when we confront him about his misbehavior.

 Notes _____

_____

_____

_____

_____

_____

 To see how this works, let's turn to the chart on page 62 of the *Parent's Guide.*

? The first column shows the parent's feeling and the second the child's response to correction. For example, if we feel annoyed with the child's behavior, and, when we correct him, he stops but starts again very soon, what's the negative approach?

- undue attention-seeking

? And what's the child's goal?

- contact

? What if you feel angry during a conflict with your child, and his response to your anger is either to escalate the misbehavior or to give in, only to fight again later? What are the negative approach and the basic goal?

- rebellion (negative approach)
- power (basic goal)

What if your child does something or says something and you feel hurt, and her response to correction is either to continue to hurt you or to escalate the misbehavior?

- revenge (negative approach)
- protection (basic goal)

 What if you feel helpless when you attempt to get through to your child and his response to correction is to become passive and refuse to try?

- undue avoidance (negative approach)
- withdrawal (basic goal)

 If you'll notice in your *Parent's Guide* on pages 62 through 65 following the chart, there are brief explanations of each of the goals, their negative approaches, and how we as parents sometimes pay off the negative approach, thus reinforcing the negative behavior. I strongly urge you to read this at home this week, so you'll have a better understanding of the model.

D. The Parent-Child Cycle

 We'll take a look at alternatives to paying off misbehavior in just a few minutes, but first I want to expand on what we have been learning. Let's go back to the think-feel-do cycle and ask ourselves what happens to that cycle when there are 2 people influencing each other—say, a parent and a child?

Child

Do

↑

Feel

↑

Think

If we take the child's think-feel-do cycle, straighten it out like this, and start at the bottom, thinking still triggers feeling and then behavior, right?

Now, let's put a parent next to that child. . . .

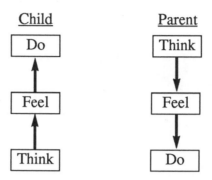

You'll notice that I put the thinking at the top for the parent, but that the arrows still show that thinking triggers feeling and doing. The reason I did this is so we can show how parents and children influence each other's cycles.

Where do you think the arrows showing how we influence each other ought to go?

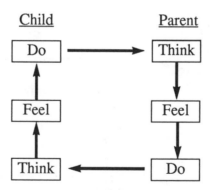

So you can see how what our children *do* influence what we think, feel and *do*, and that what we do in turn influences what they think, feel and do. And around and around it goes until we physically separate. Which is sometimes the best thing to do—especially in a power struggle.

Looking at this chart, where do you think "power" and the other goals are located?

- in the child's thinking

(Add contact, power, protection and withdrawal to the child's side of the diagram beside "Think.")

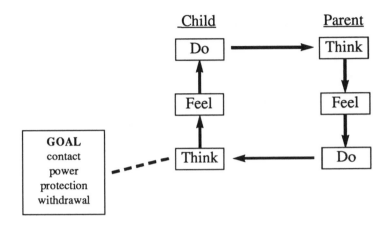

What about the child's *approach* to his goals. Where is the approach on this diagram?

- The approach is what they *do* to reach their goals, so it goes beside "Do."

(Add undue attention-seeking, rebellion, revenge and avoidance beside "Do" on the child's side.)

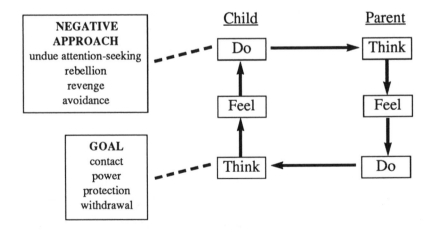

Remember, these approaches can also be positive, but since we are looking at conflicts right now, let's see how this works with a real situation. For example, think about the conflict we saw in the vignette between Dad and Janelle; let's start with Janelle's "Do." What was her misbehavior?

- refusing to clean up

PG 78 **Turning to the video practice page in your *Parent's Guide*, page 78, let's complete the cycle and start by filling in the blank marked "Misbehavior" under "Do" on the child side of the cycle.**

 (Fill in the cycle as you go so you end up with something close to the example at the end of this exercise.)

❓ And how did Janelle's behavior influence Dad's thinking? What do you think he thought about her refusal to pick up?
(Fill in cycle with something like this:)

- "She should do what I tell her because I'm the parent."
- "I'd better show her who is boss."

❓ How did he seem to feel? Annoyed? Angry? Hurt? Or hopeless? Remember, this is 1 of the 2 clues that will tell us Janelle's goal and approach.

- angry

❓ What did Dad do to try to correct Janelle's misbehavior?

- He threatened to spank her and to take away TV for a week.

❓ And how did this threat seem to influence Janelle's thinking?

- "He can control the TV, but he can't control me."

❓ And what was her feeling?

- anger

❓ How did she respond to this correction? What did she do? Remember, this is the second clue.

- She escalated the conflict: stormed out of the room.

❓ What do Dad's anger and Janelle's refusal to comply tell us about her goal and approach? Check the chart on page 62 to be sure.
 PG 62 (Fill this in also.)

- goal: power
- negative approach: rebellion

(Answer any questions briefly.)

The Parent - Child Cycle
Video # 2: Janelle - Negative

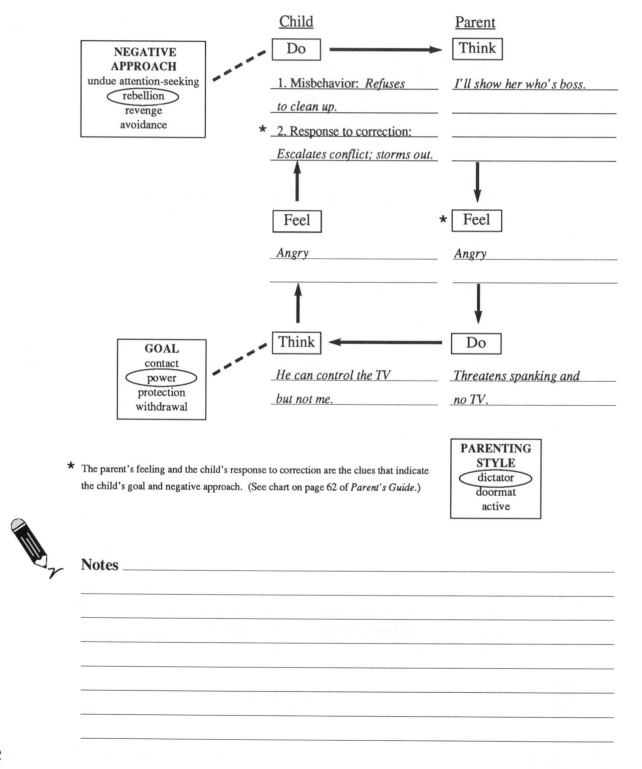

Child   Parent

NEGATIVE APPROACH
undue attention-seeking
rebellion
revenge
avoidance

Do → Think

1. Misbehavior: *Refuses to clean up.*

* 2. Response to correction: *Escalates conflict; storms out.*

I'll show her who's boss.

Feel   * Feel

Angry   *Angry*

GOAL
contact
power
protection
withdrawal

Think ← Do

He can control the TV but not me.

Threatens spanking and no TV.

PARENTING STYLE
dictator
doormat
active

* The parent's feeling and the child's response to correction are the clues that indicate the child's goal and negative approach. (See chart on page 62 of *Parent's Guide*.)

Notes _____

_____

_____

_____

_____

_____

_____

E. Power Struggles

Since we are on an example of a power struggle, let's talk about how we get in them, and how we can get out of them.

In the example of Janelle and her father, how did Dad pay off Janelle's negative approach to power? How did he let her rebellion gain her goal of power?

- He became angry and fought with her.

How does fighting with a rebellious child pay off the goal of power?

- Because to the child it looks like she "made us mad" and made us fight. It brings us down to her level. This means she is controlling our emotions, and it takes a lot of power to do that.

What is the other way to lose a power struggle—or pay off rebellion?

- We give in.

How does giving in pay off the negative approach of rebellion?

- When we give in to a child's unreasonable demands, it says to the child, "Look how powerful you are; your misbehavior got you your own way."

F. Two-Hand Push Activity

Let's do an exercise to get our adrenalin flowing. Please find a partner and stand up facing each other.
(Once everyone has a partner:)

Decide which of you will be "A" and which will be "B." Next, put your hands up like this (put hands about shoulder height up in front of you), palms out, and gently press them against your partner's hands. Now I'd like the A's to begin pushing harder against the B's. The B's do whatever they want to in response. (Wait about 5 seconds.) Okay, A's stop pushing. (Wait 5 seconds.) Now, everyone take your seats again.

What did the B's do when the A's began pushing?
(Allow sharing—particularly focusing on the natural tendency to push back when we are pushed against.)

? **And what happened when the A's stopped pushing?**
(Most of the B's will probably have stopped pushing, too.)

? **How was this like a power struggle between a parent and a child?**

- When we try to control children by being demanding, overbearing and autocratic, they are more likely to rebel and push back.
- But when we back off a little and acknowledge that they can make some of their own decisions, they are more open to our influence.

? **What are some other ways we can avoid fighting or giving in and thus avoid power struggles? Let's review the *Active Parenting Today* alternative from Session I and see what Steve and Pat did differently with Janelle.**

 ## Active Style Revisited

? **What did you notice Steven and Pat doing differently this time? How did they avoid fighting or giving in?**

- They were firm, yet still calm.
- They set clear limits, but negotiated within those limits.
- They set up a logical consequence instead of a threat of punishment (more on this next week).
- They relied on the needs of the situation and family values, instead of the wants of either the parent or the child ("The situation calls for it," not "I call for it.").

? **What else can you do to avoid or get out of a power struggle?**

- Strengthen the relationship with Family Enrichment Activities and encouragement.
- Build courage and self-esteem in your child.
- Take your sails out of the child's wind. (Sidestep the struggle for power by leaving the argument . . . when you can.)

 **Break** (10 min. _____ to _____)

84

G. Four Goals Video Practice

In this next video practice, we're going to have a chance to practice recognizing goals and mistaken approaches, as well as see how the dictator and doormat styles of parenting pay off such misbehavior. Then we'll see an example of how each parent could have used the active style of parenting to redirect the child towards the positive approach.

Please turn to page 79 in your *Parent's Guide* where you'll see the next parent-child cycle form titled "Four Goals Video Practice." After we watch the first vignette, we'll fill this out together.

(A completed form appears on page 87 of this *Leader's Guide* for your reference.)

Four Goals Video Practice: Zack - Negative

● ●

? How many of you have ever felt like Laura does right now?

? Let's see what's going on. Let's begin with the misbehavior. What is Zack *doing* that is a problem for Mother?
(Fill in this cycle as before.)

    • interrupting her phone call

Please write that beside "Misbehavior" under "Do" in the Child column.

? The arrow tells us that Zack's behavior—interrupting Mom—triggers her thinking. What do you think Laura is thinking in this vignette?
(It could be many things.)

    • "I've got to take care of Zack's needs."
    • "I wish I could finish my phone call in peace."

Please fill this in under "Think" on the parent's side.

? How does Laura seem to feel? And notice this is one of our 2 clues to Zack's goal and approach.

    • annoyed (If someone suggests "frustrated," ask whether she seems frustrated/angry or frustrated/annoyed.)

? **What does Laura do to attempt to correct Zack?**

- She keeps asking him to be quiet and finally ends the call.

? **And how does this seem to influence Zack? What do you think he is thinking?**

- "I'm keeping Mom busy with me."
- "I won't let her ignore me."

? **How does he seem to feel?**

- glad to keep her busy
- a little insecure without her

? **And finally, what does he do in response to Laura's correction—our second clue?**

- He leaves her alone for a few minutes, but then thinks of something else to distract her—playing the TV too loud.

? **What do you think is Zack's goal, and what is his negative approach to that goal? Again, you can check the chart on page 62 of your *Parent's Guide* to be sure.**

PG | 62

- goal: contact
- negative approach: undue attention-seeking

? **How could you tell using the 2 clues?**

- Mother was annoyed.
- Zack responded to correction with a start and stop behavior.

? **Finally, what was Laura's parenting style in this vignette?**

- Doormat - She let Zack take advantage of her.

? **How does her doormat style pay off Zack's misbehavior?**

- She continues to talk to him, thus giving him the contact he wants.
- She finally ends her conversation and gives him even more contact.

Notes _____

_____

_____

_____

Four Goals Video Practice
Video # 4: Zack - Negative

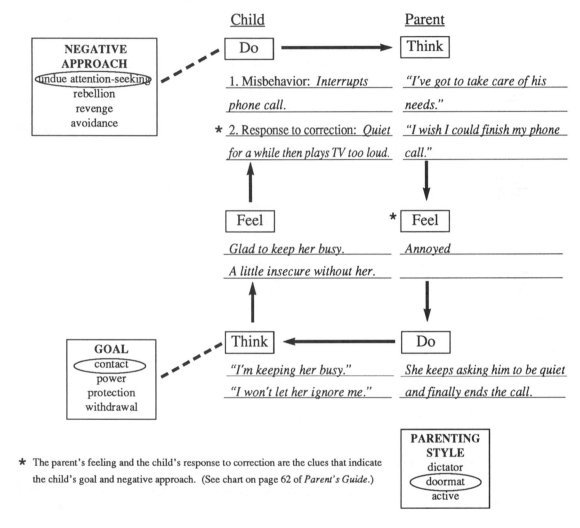

Child   Parent

NEGATIVE APPROACH
~~undue attention-seeking~~
rebellion
revenge
avoidance

| Do | → | Think |

1. Misbehavior: *Interrupts phone call.*

"I've got to take care of his needs."

* 2. Response to correction: *Quiet for a while then plays TV too loud.*

"I wish I could finish my phone call."

| Feel | * | Feel |

Glad to keep her busy.
A little insecure without her.

Annoyed

GOAL
~~contact~~
power
protection
withdrawal

| Think | ← | Do |

"I'm keeping her busy."
"I won't let her ignore me."

She keeps asking him to be quiet and finally ends the call.

PARENTING STYLE
dictator
~~doormat~~
active

* The parent's feeling and the child's response to correction are the clues that indicate the child's goal and negative approach. (See chart on page 62 of *Parent's Guide*.)

(Note: This is an example. Other words may also be correct.)

Now, remember that there is nothing wrong with a child wanting contact with his mother. Let's see how Laura might have used the active style of parenting to redirect him towards more positive ways of achieving this goal. See what she does differently.

Notes _____

_____

_____

Four Goals Video Practice: Zack - Active

Before we talk about what Laura did differently, let me say that you are probably aware that there are many ways a child such as Zack might have responded at the end of the vignette. What if Zack continued to interrupt? What if he had a tantrum? What if he ran out of the house? What if he hung up the phone? Later—*after* we've explored more of the techniques of *Active Parenting Today*—it might be fun to go back and play some of these "what ifs" and see how we might respond. But for right now, we're trying to keep it simple so that you can begin seeing some of these techniques in action.

So, what did you notice that Laura did differently?

- She was firmer.
- She gave him a choice.
- She set a limit: No interrupting for 10 minutes.
- She gave him an opportunity to have *contact* with her later by using what we call a "when-then" choice.
- She used a timer to help him monitor the situation. Timers, by the way, are great, especially with young children. If you don't have one, I really recommend your getting one.

Let's take a look at the next situation.

Four Goals Video Practice: Jade - Negative

(Lead the group in filling out the Parent-Child Cycle on page 80 in the *Parent's Guide* as before, using the following questions or the previously completed cycle.)

Let's see if you can figure out what is going on with Jade. To begin, what was Jade doing . . . and for that matter, not doing?

- Sitting by herself; not trying to make friends

Let's put this beside "Misbehavior" on the cycle. This is not misbehavior in the sense that Jade needs discipline, but it is "mistaken" behavior.
(Continue to board bulleted answers.)

? **And what did Kathi seem to think about this?**

- She should be out making friends.
- I need to push her to go make friends.
- I don't know what else to do.

? **How did Kathi seem to feel at the end there?**

- hopeless

? **What did she do to change Jade's behavior?**

- She tried to push Jade into going next door.

? **What did Jade seem to think about this?**

- I can't make friends.
- Nobody likes me.
- I give up.

? **How did she seem to feel?**

- sad, lonely

? **What was her response to Kathi's efforts?**

- She became more discouraged and gave up.

? **What were her goal and mistaken approach?**

- goal: withdrawal
- negative approach: avoidance

? **How do you know?**
(Refer to chart on page 62 of *Parent's Guide*.)

PG | 62

- Kathi's feeling of *helplessness*
- Jade's refusal to try

? **What was Kathi's style of parenting?**

- Dictator - Rather than accept Jade's feelings, she tried to coerce her into getting over her fears all at once.

? **How did she eventually pay off Jade's approach of avoidance?**

- She gave up.

Four Goals Video Practice
Video # 6: Jade - Negative

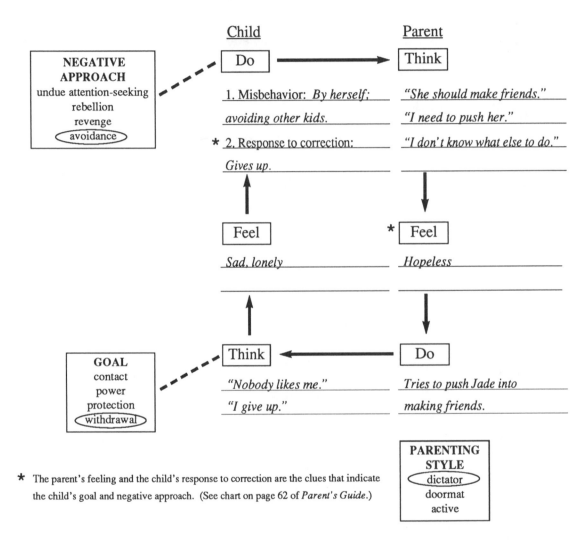

	Child	Parent
	Do	**Think**
NEGATIVE APPROACH undue attention-seeking, rebellion, revenge, (avoidance)	1. Misbehavior: *By herself; avoiding other kids.*	*"She should make friends." "I need to push her."*
	* 2. Response to correction: *Gives up.*	*"I don't know what else to do."*
	Feel	* **Feel**
	Sad, lonely	*Hopeless*
GOAL contact, power, protection, (withdrawal)	**Think** *"Nobody likes me." "I give up."*	**Do** *Tries to push Jade into making friends.*
		PARENTING STYLE (dictator), doormat, active

* The parent's feeling and the child's response to correction are the clues that indicate the child's goal and negative approach. (See chart on page 62 of *Parent's Guide*.)

(Note: This is an example. Other words may also be correct.)

Now, let's see how Kathi could use an active approach to begin redirecting Jade to overcome her fears rather than give into them.

Notes _____

_____

_____

_____

_____

What does Kathi do differently this time?

- She is much more empathetic—caring about Jade.
- She listens to her feelings—even names them.
- Her suggestions are more gentle.
- She doesn't press but backs off when she meets resistance.
- She finds a step Jade is ready to take and encourages her that little bit.

 Before we watch this last example, let me ask you a question. How many of you have 2 or more children?

 How many of them ever fight with each other?

 Can you ever be really sure how those fights start?

This vignette may look familiar.

 # 8   ## *Four Goals Video Practice: Ramon - Negative*

 PG | 81

(If you have time, you can lead the group through the cycle on page 81 as before, using the completed cycle that follows. To save time, or with groups who you feel are not ready for the Parent-Child Cycle, you can use the following questions instead of the cycle. This simpler technique can also be used with the earlier examples.)

 Let's take a look at this one. First, how is Dad feeling right now?

- hurt

 And how did Ramon respond to his attempts at correction?

- He escalated the fight: "I hate you."

? Using these two clues and the chart on page 62 of your *Parent's Guide*, what is Ramon's negative approach?

PG 62

- revenge

? And what goal is his revenge aimed at achieving?

- protection

? What is Dad's style of parenting?

- dictator

? What is the payoff to Ramon from this dictator style?

- It justifies to Ramon his right to get even: "You hurt me, so I have a right to hurt you back."

Notes _____

_____

_____

_____

_____

_____

_____

_____

_____

_____

_____

_____

_____

_____

_____

_____

_____

_____

_____

Four Goals Video Practice
Video # 8: Ramon - Negative

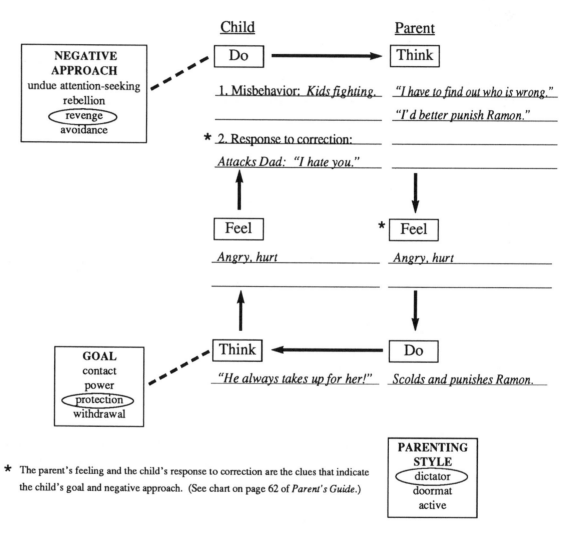

Child   Parent

| NEGATIVE APPROACH |
| undue attention-seeking |
| rebellion |
| *revenge* |
| avoidance |

Do → Think

1. Misbehavior: *Kids fighting.*   *"I have to find out who is wrong."*

"I'd better punish Ramon."

* 2. Response to correction:

Attacks Dad: "I hate you."

Feel   * Feel

Angry, hurt   *Angry, hurt*

| GOAL |
| contact |
| power |
| *protection* |
| withdrawal |

Think ← Do

"He always takes up for her!"   *Scolds and punishes Ramon.*

| PARENTING STYLE |
| *dictator* |
| doormat |
| active |

* The parent's feeling and the child's response to correction are the clues that indicate the child's goal and negative approach. (See chart on page 62 of *Parent's Guide*.)

(Note: This is an example. Other words may also be correct.)

Now, let's see how José could use an active style of parenting to avoid getting sucked into his stepchildren's fight.

Notes _____

_____

_____

_____

Four Goals Video Practice: Ramon - Active

 What did you notice that José did differently that time?

- He didn't blow up at Ramon.
- He didn't rescue Sara; he "stimulated independence" by encouraging her to handle it herself.
- He offered support by agreeing to hold a Family Council Meeting that afternoon.

The Family Council Meeting is a terrific method of family problem solving that we'll learn in Session 6.

 What else could a parent do to avoid getting into the middle of a fight?

- Separate the two children: "You can either handle this without hitting or yelling or you can go to separate areas until you can."

III. Four Goals at Home (15 min. _____ to _____)

A. Analyzing the Problem Activity

 Now it's time to apply what we've been learning to your own families. (◣ **If you're using goal cards: Please pick a problem from your goal card for one of your children that you would like to work on.) Now turn to page 82 in your *Parent's Guide* and fill in the questions:**

- **What is the misbehavior?**
- **What did you do to attempt to correct it?**
- **How did your child respond to your correction?**
- **How did you feel during the conflict?**

 Then use the chart on page 62 to find out:

- **What goal was your child trying to achieve?**
- **What was his negative approach?**
- **How did you pay off the negative approach?**
  (Wait a few minutes.)

Now please get with a partner (or your buddies) for a few minutes and discuss what you came up with.
(Allow about 5 minutes.)

Are there any questions or comments?

How many of your children had an approach of undue attention-seeking?

How many had rebellion—a power struggle?

Any revenge?

Any avoidance?
(Note which approaches had the most hands so you can focus on these in later sessions.)

B. Four Goals at Home Observation

This week at home I'd like you to observe how this Parent-Child Cycle happens, particularly how you get hooked into old patterns of responding—anger and punishment—or giving in. Especially be aware of how this pays off your child's negative approach and influences the misbehavior to continue.

Don't worry about solving the problem this week. We'll be learning some of the discipline skills you saw tonight in the next session, so be sure not to miss that one. And if you are dying to try out some of these techniques at home this week, *please be sure to read Chapter 4 first.*

Notes _____

_____

_____

_____

_____

_____

_____

_____

_____

_____

_____

IV. Family Enrichment Activity: Teaching Skills

(5 min. _____ to _____)

Now, since part of redirecting any misbehavior is dependent on your relationship with your child, let's look at this week's Family Enrichment Activity.

 # 10 *Family Enrichment Activity: Teaching Skills*

Are there any questions about this week's activity?

How can you tell what your child is interested in learning?

- Talk to her.
- Observe what he seems interested in doing.

PG 76-77 You'll notice in your *Parent's Guide* on pages 76 and 77 the tips Dr. Popkin mentioned, as well as a guide sheet for you to complete for next week's Share And Tell. (◢ You'll also want to be sure to call your buddy as usual to see how it's going and to offer encouragement.)

V. Video Review (3 min. _____ to _____)

It's time to play our video review.

Notes _____

_____

_____

_____

_____

_____

_____

_____

_____

_____

Video Review

• •

VI. Home Activities (2 min. _____ to _____)

PG | 83 **Please turn to page 83 in your *Parent's Guide* and notice the Home Activites for this week:**

HOME ACTIVITIES

1. **Read Chapter 3 in your *Parent's Guide*. If you wish to read ahead, please do so.**
2. **Teach a skill to each child (or begin teaching) and complete the Family Enrichment Activity guide sheet on page 77.**
3. **Call your buddy (optional).**

And continue:

- **"Every day a little play."**
- **Encourage, encourage, encourage.**

Great! Have a terrific week, and whatever you do, don't miss Session 4!

Notes _____

_____

_____

_____

_____

_____

_____

_____

_____

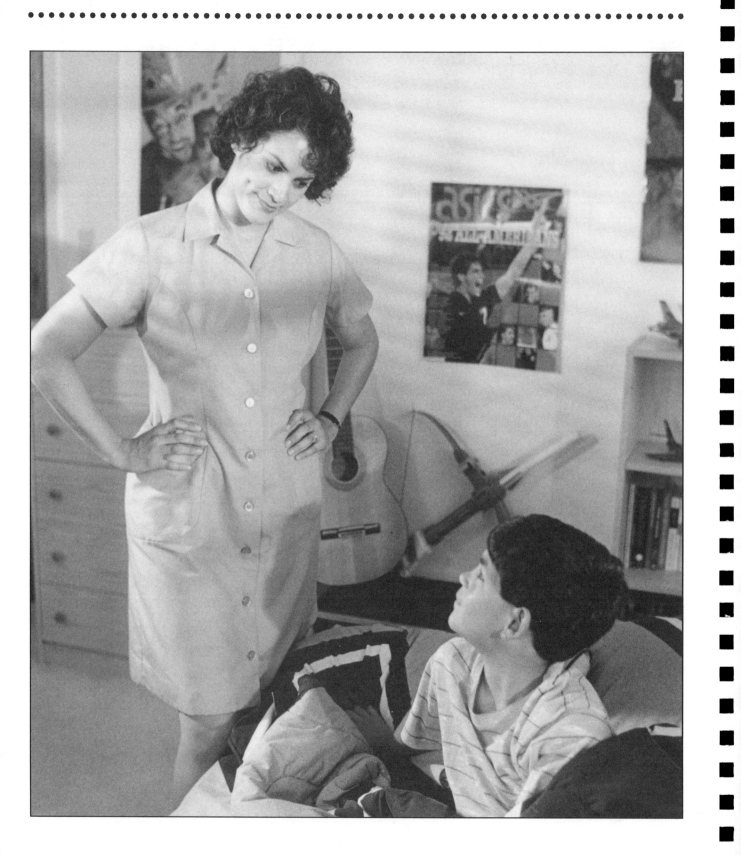

SESSION 4
DEVELOPING RESPONSIBILITY

	Topic	Activity	Video
I	Share And Tell		1. Share And Tell (2:25)
II	Responsibility		
III	Responsibility And Problem Handling	Who Owns The Problem Video Practice	2. Whose Problem Is This Anyway? (2:18) 3. Who Owns The Problem Video Practice (1:59) 4. Mutual Respect (2:08)
IV	"I" Messages		5. "I" Messages (3:50)
V	Natural And Logical Consequences	Remember When Activity: Natural Consequences (optional) Logical Consequences Video Practice Logical Consequences	6. "The Butterfly's Wings" (:51) 7. Natural Consequences (3:20) 8. Logical Consequences (1:53) 9. Logical Consequences Video Practice (6:30)
VI	Family Enrichment Activity: Positive "I" Messages		10. Family Enrichment Activity: Positive "I" Messages (1:36)
VII	Video Review		11. Video Review (1:02)
VIII	Home Activities		

OBJECTIVES FOR SESSION 4:

- Define responsibility and the role of choice and consequence in developing responsibility.
- Present a model for handling problems in a family.
- Be able to construct an "I" message.
- Understand and be able to apply natural and logical consequences.
- Understand the importance of mutual respect in dealing with children.

I. Share And Tell (10 min. _____ to _____)

Welcome to Session 4 of *Active Parenting Today,* "Developing Responsibility." This is the session when we'll be learning some effective discipline methods. But, before we do, let's see how things went at home this week.

Who has a success to share?
(Allow 2 or 3 successes, using them to talk about the home assignments and other skills that have been covered. If any home assignments are missed, you can ask:)

How did it go with your Four Goals Home Observation Activity? Please turn to page 82 in your *Parent's Guide* and see what you wrote down. Did you notice yourself paying off mistaken approaches, or by observing the Parent-Child Cycle, did things change in some way?
(Allow brief sharing.)

PG | 82

Now turn in your *Parent's Guide* to page 77 and see how your Family Enrichment Activity went.

PG | 77

Who had a success teaching a skill you would like to share?

Who had a problem we can learn from?

Now, let's watch our Share And Tell video, and see how Diane and Stephanie are doing.

Share And Tell

  Any thoughts or comments?

  How did Diane sidestep the struggle for power?

- She caught herself getting angry and backed off a little.
- She used "parent judo"—like the Two-Hand Push Activity we did last week.
- She shared why growing things was important to her, without pushing it on Stephanie: She "sold, not told."

(This is a good time to evaluate the buddy system and make any corrections that will help.)

II. Responsibility (5 min. _____ to _____)

A. What Is Responsibility?

Responsibility is one of those often misunderstood concepts. Some people view it as blame, while many have difficulty determining when responsibility begins and ends.

How would you define responsibility?
(Accept all answers.)

In a nutshell, *Active Parenting Today* defines responsibility as "accepting that what happens to us in our lives (the consequences) results from the choices we make."

Responsibility = Choice + Consequences

What is the advantage of being responsible?

- When we recognize that the consequences in our lives come from the choices we make, we have more control over our lives and learn to make better choices.
- When we blame our consequences on others or make excuses for our consequences, we don't learn to make better choices.

- Children who learn to accept responsibility for their own thinking, feeling and doing eventually get into success cycles because they learn from their failures.

Notes _____

_____

_____

_____

_____

_____

B. Avoiding Responsibility

Given this advantage, why do people sometimes avoid responsibility?

- fear of being wrong and blamed
- fear of punishment
- fear of being put down

Punishment = Discipline

Let's talk about punishment for a minute.

Is discipline the same as punishment?

- No

Punishment ≠ Discipline!

Discipline comes from the Latin word "to teach," and there are many positive ways to teach, as we'll see.

Punishment is *one* way to discipline, but it is a negative way that implies hurting the child or at least causing the child pain.

What are some examples of punishments?

- taking away privileges
- taking away possessions
- grounding

- scolding
- withdrawing affection
- spanking

 If you remember our Punishment Activity in Session I, why don't punishments work in the long run?

- In a democratic society, when you hurt someone, he perceives a right to hurt you back.
- Punishments lead to power struggles and retaliation.
- They may teach that "might makes right."
- The child's fear of punishment can lead to fear of the punisher. This leads to a negative parent-child relationship.
- The child learns to avoid punishment by using blame and justifying, instead of positive behavior.

We'll come back to discipline in a minute, but first let's talk about problems in families.

III. Responsibility And Problem Handling (20 min._____ to _____)

A. Who Owns The Problem?

Every family is going to have problems and conflicts. Rather than looking at these as negative events, we can think of them as opportunities for teaching responsibility, cooperation and courage.

Our experience has shown that the biggest obstacle in handling problems successfully is not knowing whose responsibility it is to find a solution. Or as we say in this program, not knowing "who owns the problem."

Let's look at several videos to get a better idea of this concept.

 Notes _____

_____

_____

_____

_____

Whose Problem Is This Anyway?

PG | 90

Let's turn in our *Parent's Guide* to page 90, and look at the clues for determining who owns the problem. What are some things to look for? *write these on board for parents to refer to*

- With whom is the problem behavior directly interfering?
- ✱ • Who is raising the issue or making the complaint?
- Whose goals are being blocked?

In the case of Gloria and Ramon, who owns the problem?

- Gloria

Why?

- It's her goal of having Ramon get up on time that is blocked. She is making the complaint.

By the way, what's her style of parenting?

- Doormat - She is pampering Ramon by being his personal wake-up service.

In terms of Pat and Janelle, whose problem is this?

- Janelle, because she got the extra homework. She is making the complaint.

B. Who Owns The Problem Video Practice

Now that you're getting the idea of problem ownership, let's practice identifying whose problem it is.

PG | 111

I'm going to show you 4 different vignettes, and after each vignette I'll ask you to jot down on page 111 of your *Parent's Guide* whose problem you think it is.

Okay, let's see how you perceive these scenes. Here's the first one:

Notes _____

_____

Who Owns The Problem Video Practice

(After each vignette, allow time for the class to make entries. Also, discuss ownership and reason. If there is any disagreement, have the class discuss it for clarification. Repeat the process until all 4 vignettes have been shown.)

Scene 1. Laura and Zack - Phone

Who owns the problem?

- Laura

Why?

- Her goal of talking on the phone is being interfered with.

Scene 2. Laura and Zack - Shoes

Who owns the problem?

- Zack

Why?

- He has responsibility for keeping up with his own shoes. His goal of having his shoes is blocked.

Scene 3. Kathi and Jade - Swing

Who owns the problem?

- Jade

Why?

- She has the upset feelings. She has a responsibility to make friends.

Scene 4. José, Ramon and Sara - Kicking

? Who owns the problem?

- the kids

? Why?

- Children have a responsibility to handle their own relationships. Ramon's goal of sitting peacefully on the sofa is being blocked. Sara has the upset feelings and is making the complaint.

Now for Scene 5, I'd like you to jot down a recent conflict you've had with one of your children, and determine who owned the problem.
(After participants fill out Scene 5, share results.)

- Have parents generate their own examples of ownership to clarify understanding

Who Owns The Problem Video Practice

Scene 1. Laura and Zack - Phone
Who owns the problem? *Laura.*
Why? *Her goal of talking on the phone is being interferred with.*

Scene 2. Laura and Zack - Shoes
Who owns the problem? *Zack.*
Why? *His goal of having his shoes is blocked.*

Scene 3. Kathi and Jade - Swing
Who owns the problem? *Jade.*
Why? *She has the responsibility to handle making friends.*

Scene 4. José, Ramon and Sara - Kicking
Who owns the problem? *The kids.*
Why? *Children have the responsibility to handle their own relationships.*

Scene 5. A Problem With Your Own Family
Who owns the problem? _____

Why? _____

_____

_____

_____

_____

_____

_____

C. The Problem-Handling Model

Once we determine who owns the problem, we have a better idea about how to handle the problem. If you'll turn in your *Parent's Guide* to page 89, you'll notice a model for handling problems in a family.

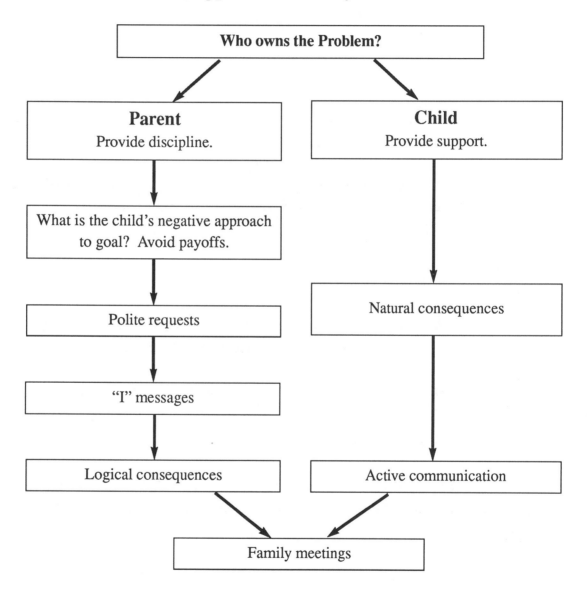

Who owns the Problem?

Parent
Provide discipline.

Child
Provide support.

What is the child's negative approach to goal? Avoid payoffs.

Polite requests

Natural consequences

"I" messages

Logical consequences

Active communication

Family meetings

ENCOURAGE ... ENCOURAGE ... ENCOURAGE.

Notice that once we determine who owns the problem, there are 2 sides to the model: the parent's side and the child's side. When the parent owns the problem, it's a case for discipline. When the child owns the problem, our role is to provide support. The skills that we use for these 2 main roles of parenting are similar, but different. What are the skills we can rely on when the parent owns the problem?

- Polite requests
- "I" messages
- Logical consequences
- Family meetings

During this session we'll be looking at the first 3 of these: polite requests, "I" messages and logical consequences.

 What skills do we use when our child owns the problem, like in the situation between Pat and Janelle, and we want to offer support?

- Natural consequences
- Active communication
- Family meetings

We'll cover natural consequences this week, active communication during Session 5, and talk about family meetings in Session 6.

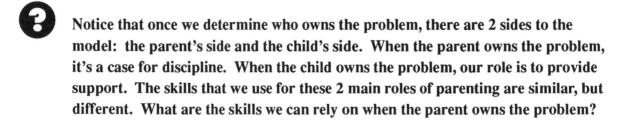 If you think of this problem-handling model as an engine, the fuel this engine runs on is . . .

- encouragement

That's right, no matter what we do as parents—discipline or support—it won't work unless we add lots of encouragement and build on strengths.

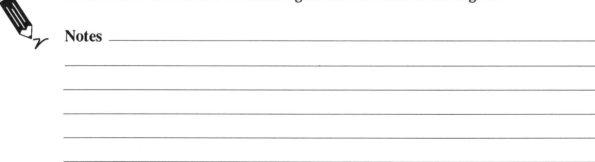 Notes _____

_____

_____

_____

_____

_____

_____

D. Mutual Respect

When we think about discipline, we think about setting limits on our children's behavior—restricting some of their freedom. How we do this in a democratic society is a very sensitive issue—one that revolves around a concept made famous in a song by Aretha Franklin a number of years ago. Does anyone remember that concept?

R-E-S-P-E-C-T

In fact, we now talk of respect being a two-way street between parents and children. So it is more appropriate to talk about mutual respect.

Mutual respect

Let's see what the next video has to say about this important aspect of parenting relations.

 Mutual Respect

● ●

Are there any questions or comments about the section on mutual respect? Let's keep this concept of mutual respect in mind as we continue talking about methods of disciplining our children.

IV. "I" Messages (15 min. _____ to _____)

We said the first step in getting a child to change behavior is simply to ask politely. The next video demonstrates this with Gloria and Ramon, and then goes on to show a firmer technique that we refer to as "I" messages. Let's take a look.

Notes _____

_____

_____

_____

_____

 # 5 **"I" Messages**

 Okay, does anyone have questions about "I" messages? Do you think you could construct an "I" message?

Let's try an example together. Let's say your 10-year-old has been playing loudly for the past 15 minutes and you have a terrible headache. Let's also say you've asked him politely to play quietly, but somehow he has gotten loud again. Take a minute and write an "I" message you might use to let him know how you feel and what you'd like.

 I have a problem with _____

I feel _____

Because _____

I would like _____

 Turn to page 112 in your *Parent's Guide* and construct your "I" message.
(Allow 1 or 2 minutes, then share a couple of the "I" messages, providing feedback.)

Now, on the same page in your *Parent's Guide*, there is a place for you to jot down a problem you own with one of your children. Let's take a few minutes to jot down the problem, and then in the space provided write an "I" message you can use the next time the problem comes up.
(Allow 2 or 3 minutes, then ask the parents to pair up and share the "I" messages, giving feedback and encouragement to each other. If you have time, ask for several to be shared with the group. Make sure everyone has constructed an "I" message to try at home this week.)

 Break (10 min.____ to ____)

 Notes _____

V. Natural And Logical Consequences (50 min.____ to ____)

A. Consequences

 Referring back to the Problem-Handling Model, what's the next step on the discipline side when "I" messages are not effective?

- logical consequences

One important lesson psychologists have learned over the past generations is that the choices we make are affected by the consequences that follow.

Let's see what this means.

 ### "The Butterfly's Wings"

 How does this story relate to the idea of consequences?

- Consequences help our children strengthen their wings.
- They stimulate independence; our "overprotecting" does not.

Basically, there are two types of consequences:

1. Those that circumstances provide without our help as parents . . .

 Natural consequences

2. And those that we as parents provide to teach our children what logically follows their choice to misbehave.

 Logical consequences

B. Natural Consequences

Let's take a look at the first type of consequences, what we call natural consequences.

Natural consequences

The results that naturally occur from a child's behavior without the parent doing anything.

Let's hear more about natural consequences from Dr. Popkin, and see an example.

 ## Natural Consequences

• •

Let's review. What were the natural consequences of Janelle's decision to leave her skates outside?

- Her skates were ruined.

Did Mother have to do anything for this consequence to occur?

- No

What might have happened if Mom had lectured at this point or blamed or otherwise scolded Janelle?

- Janelle may have become resentful and not learned from the consequences.

 Remember: When children don't feel respected, they tend to misbehave.

Notes _____

_____

_____

_____

_____

_____

_____

_____

_____

_____

_____

C. Remember When Activity: Natural Consequences

We've all learned many of life's lessons through the natural consequences of our behavior. Let's close our eyes for a minute and think back to our own childhood years and some of the lessons we learned through consequences provided by Mother Nature or circumstances other than those controlled by our parents. (Allow 30-40 seconds.)

 Who would like to share something you learned through natural consequences? (Allow 2-3 examples.)

So, sometimes the best thing to do as a parent is just stay out of the way and let the natural consequences do the teaching. Of course, a parent may want to offer support, and we'll look at some ways in the next session when we talk about active communication.

 Notes _____

_____

_____

_____

_____

_____

_____

_____

_____

_____

_____

_____

_____

_____

_____

_____

_____

_____

D. When Not To Use Natural Consequences

There are times when the natural consequences do have limitations. What are some situations when we wouldn't want the natural consequences to do the teaching?

1. when the situation is too dangerous

What's an example of this?

- swimming without supervision . . . drowning
- riding a bike on a busy street . . . getting hit by a car

2. when the consequences are too distant

What's an example here?

- not brushing your teeth . . . tooth decay
- not keeping up with schoolwork . . . dropping out or at least not having as many options for college or work later

3. when the natural consequences do not affect the child

And what's an example of this?

- child runs in a grocery store . . . knocks over groceries and disturbs other shoppers
- child throws a ball in the house . . . breaks your lamp

E. Logical Consequences

When "I" messages aren't strong enough to motivate a child to change behavior, and there are no natural consequences that fit the situation, then we want to use the second type of consequences—logical consequences.

Logical Consequences
> Those results a parent provides to teach children what logically follows when they violate family rules or the needs of a situation.

Why do you think they are called "logical consequences"?

- Because the consequence is logically connected to the misbehavior.

Let's see what Zack and Dr. Popkin have to show us about logical consequences.

Logical Consequences

Let's see what's going on here.

What was Zack's misbehavior?

- writing on the walls with crayons

And what does Laura's feeling of annoyance and Zack's response to correction tell you about his goal and mistaken approach?

- Her annoyance and his stopping suggest a goal of contact and a mistaken approach of undue attention-seeking.

What are some typical punishments she thinks about using?

- sitting in the corner
- a spanking
- no TV

What do they have to do with writing on the walls?

- Nothing. They aren't logical.

What is the logical consequence Laura comes up with?

- for Zack to wash it off the walls

Why is this logical?

- He messed up, so he should be the one to clean up.

Does this pay off his mistaken approach of undue attention-seeking?

- not if Laura doesn't lecture or nag or stand there and supervise

Do children like logical consequences?

- No. In fact they sometimes prefer punishment, like Zack preferred sitting in the corner. But they see them as more fair and are more likely to cooperate with them.

F. Logical Consequences vs. Punishment

Let's look at some of the differences between logical consequences and punishment.

	Logical Consequence	Punishment
Connection		
Parent's Goal		
Tone of Voice		

What's the connection between the misbehavior and a logical consequence or a punishment?

(Add the words "logical result" and "not related" in the previous diagram beside "Connection.")

- Logical consequences are logical results of the child's misbehavior.
- Punishments are not related to the misbehavior.

Who would like to give us an example?
(Encourage class to give several examples.)

The second factor has to do with the parent's goal. Too often we only focus on the behavior and miss looking at the person's intention.

For the parent's goal, what do you think is the difference between a logical consequence and punishment?
(Accept all answers.)

They are both intended to teach; however . . .

- Logical consequences focus on teaching *responsible behavior*.
- Punishment focuses on teaching *blind obedience*.

(Add the words "responsible behavior" and "blind obedience" in the appropriate columns of the diagram.)

How about some examples of what that means?
(Accept and clarify class responses.)

 How do you think the tone would differ?
(Accept all answers.)

- Logical consequence: firm, but calm, without anger and hostility.

 (Add "firm, but calm.")

- Punishment: tone contains anger, resentment, sarcasm or threat.

 (Add "angry.")

	Logical Consequence	Punishment
Connection	logical result	not related
Parent's Goal	responsible behavior	blind obedience
Tone of Voice	firm, but calm	angry

G. Logical Consequences Video Practice

To help us practice thinking in terms of logical consequences, let's work on a Video Practice.

I'm going to play 5 situational vignettes. In each situation the parent owns the problem, but in trying to correct the problem, the parent makes a mistake using logical consequences by violating one of these 8 guidelines.
(Either board the guidelines or have group turn to page 106 in the *Parent's Guide*.)

Notes _____

_____

_____

_____

_____

_____

Logical consequences guidelines

1. Give the child a choice.
   - either/or choice
   - when/then choice
2. Ask the child to help.
3. Make sure the consequence is logical.
4. Give choices you can live with.
5. Keep your tone firm and calm.
6. Give choice once, then act.
7. Expect testing. Follow through.
8. Allow the child to try again later.

Let's take a few moments to go over these guidelines.
(Go over with the group, giving examples as necessary.)

 Are there any questions about these 8 guidelines?

 Please turn to page 113 in your *Parent's Guide* where you'll find a guide sheet for this activity. We will be pausing the tape throughout to identify mistakes the parents make and then to come up with our own logical consequences. Let's watch the first scene and see if we can tell which guideline or guidelines Gloria violates.

 ## Logical Consequences Video Practice

• •

(At the first "Pause" message . . .)

 Which of the logical consequences guidelines did Mother violate?
(Allow a few seconds for parents to write their answers on the guide sheet. This reinforces their learning. Note: If you have time, you might have them work in pairs or small groups to arrive at their answers.)

- Ask the child to help.
- Make sure the consequence is logical.

 Now, what might be a logical consequence that Gloria could use? Remember,

118

there is no *one* right answer. There are as many logical consequences as we can creatively come up with. We then use our knowledge of the child and her goals to decide on the one that might work best.
(Allow group to brainstorm 2-3 logical consequences. Don't worry if they don't come up with the example on the video.)

We came up with some good possibilities. Now let's see the example given on the video. And remember, this isn't the *right* answer, it's *an* answer.

(Continue playing the video, which will conclude Scene 1 and continue on to Scene 2. Pause tape when indicated and use the following completed guide sheet as your reference.)

 Notes _____

_____

_____

_____

_____

_____

_____

_____

_____

_____

_____

_____

_____

_____

_____

_____

_____

_____

_____

_____

_____

Logical Consequences Video Practice Guide Sheet

Problem	Guideline Violated	Possible Logical Consequence
Scene 1. Ramon oversleeping	Ask the child to help. Make sure the consequence is logical.	Either get up on time or go to bed an hour earlier.
Scene 2. Ramon oversleeping	Expect testing. Give the choice one time, then act.	Ramon must go to bed an hour early tonight.
Scene 3. Janelle skating in street	Give the child a choice. Keep your tone firm and calm.	Either skate on the sidewalk or driveway *or* lose skates for a week.
Scene 4. Ben not eating his peas	Only give choices you can live with.	When you have finished your dinner, you may have dessert.
Scene 5. Jade not returning art supplies	Allow the child to try again later.	Either return my art supplies or lose their use for a period. ("You can try again later.")

 Notes _____

_____

_____

_____

_____

_____

_____

_____

H. Logical Consequences Activity

Let's take some time now to see how you can use logical consequences at home this week to help you handle a problem with one of your own children. Please turn to page 114 in your *Parent's Guide* and jot down a problem in the space provided that you would like to work on.
(Allow 1 or 2 minutes.)

As you've probably noticed, it's not always easy to come up with a logical consequence. Punishment is a lot easier—but it doesn't work as well in the long run. With some practice, you'll find it gets easier and easier to think of logical consequences.

To help you with your first one, how about teaming up with a partner (◢ or your buddy), and see if you can come up with a good logical consequence for each of you. If you need some help, call me over.
(Go from group to group while they are working to make sure everyone is on the right track. Allow about 10 minutes, or enough time for everyone to have a logical consequence.)

Does everyone have a logical consequence to try at home this week?
(If you have time you might have 2-3 people share their logical consequences with the group. If someone has trouble thinking of a logical consequence, you can have the large group brainstorm with them. Remember, the parent who owns the problem must agree on the logical consequence.)

Now that everyone has a logical consequence, remember you might not use it. When you sit down to talk with your child about the problem, he may help you come up with a different consequence. But you always want to have one in mind just in case.

Okay, is everyone willing to try it this week?

Great! And what are mistakes for?

- learning

Right, so don't worry if it doesn't go exactly right this first time. We'll talk it over next week and see what we can learn. And don't forget about testing!

Your kids may test to see if you follow through. So don't be surprised if the misbehavior gets worse before it gets better.

Notes _____
_____
_____
_____
_____

VI. Family Enrichment Activity: Positive "I" Messages

(5 min. _____ to _____)

I know we have covered a lot of new material this week, but it's important to continue with your Family Enrichment Activities.

- Every day a little play.
- Reaching by teaching.
- Put it in writing.

For this week's activity, we'll be looking at something we call *positive* "I" messages. Let's take a look.

 ## Family Enrichment Activity: Positive "I" Messages

• •

PG | 110   If you'll turn in your *Parent's Guide* to page 110, you'll see a place to construct a positive "I" message of your own. Look for an opportunity to connect it to the problem you're working on with your logical consequence so you can "catch em doing good."

VII. Video Review (3 min. _____ to _____)

Now, it's time for our Video Review.

122

Video Review

• •

VIII. Home Activities (2 min. _____ to _____)

 Please turn in your *Parent's Guide* to page 115 so we can go over the Home Activities for this week.

HOME ACTIVITIES

1. Read Chapter 4 in your *Parent's Guide* before trying the discipline skills. If you wish to read ahead, please do so.
2. Practice the Family Enrichment Activity: Use a positive "I" message, on page 110.
3. Try an "I" message, and fill in the guide sheet on page 112.
4. Talk about your problem with your child, and apply a logical consequence. Complete the guide sheet for that on page 114.
5. Be aware of speaking respectfully to your children this week.
6. Call your buddy (optional).

Notes _____

_____

_____

_____

_____

_____

_____

_____

_____

SESSION 5
WINNING COOPERATION

	Topic	Activity	Video
I	**Share And Tell**		1. Share And Tell (4:40)
II	**Cooperation**		2. "The Brown Flower With The Green Stem." (2:30)
III	**Communication**	Mixed Messages Communication Blocks	3. Communication Blocks (3:34)
IV	**Active Communication**	Responding to Feelings Video Practice Role-Playing Active Communication (optional)	4. Active Communication (3:46) 5. Responding to Feelings Video Practice (1:55)
V	**Family Enrichment Activity: Bedtime Routines And I Love You's**		6. Family Enrichment Activity: Bedtime Routines And I Love You's (3:26)
VI	**Video Review**		7. Video Review (:42)
VII	**Home Activities**		

OBJECTIVES FOR SESSION 5:

- Define cooperation.
- Understand problem handling when it's the child's problem.
- Sensitize the group to avoiding communication blocks.
- Begin to develop active communication skills.

I. Share And Tell (30 min. _____ to _____)

Welcome to our next-to-last session. We'll be talking about the important concepts of cooperation, communication and problem solving. But first, let's see how things went at home this week.

 Please turn in your *Parent's Guide* to page 110 and review your use of positive "I" messages.

Who has a success to share about using "I" messages or natural or logical consequences to solve a problem?
(Share and discuss.)

Who ran into a problem we can all learn from?
(Share and discuss.)

Are there any other questions concerning these skills?

Remember, it takes practice to become comfortable with a new skill, so don't give up. Keep talking to each other, and keep using these techniques.

Now, how about the concept of mutual respect? Who can share an experience when you were conscious of showing respect to a child?
(Encourage sharing.)

 Let's see how Diane Davidson did with her Home Activities.

Notes _____

_____

_____

Before you say anything, remember guideline #4 for logical consequences: Only give choices you can live with. If serving dinner on a bare table isn't something you could do, then think of another logical consequence—"do the unexpected" in a different way.

 Having said that, are there any other comments about this vignette?

What about the situation with Kyle? Have any of you noticed the same thing in your family—as one child starts improving, another starts misbehaving? (Allow discussion, encouraging participants to stick with the program for all their children as Diane has decided to do, and to let their kids know there is room in the family for two—or however many children they have—"good" kids.)

II. Cooperation (8 min. _____ to _____)

A. Cooperation Defined

The focus of this session is winning cooperation from our children. Our approach will be on how parents' communication and problem-handling skills either encourage or discourage cooperation.

So, to begin with, what does the word "cooperation" really mean? I'll give you a hint.

Co operation
(Accept all answers.)

We might sum this up with the following definition:

Two or more people working together in a mutually supportive manner for a common goal.

 Notes _____

B. Cooperation And Problem Handling

 Since one of the best opportunities to teach cooperation is when problems come up, let's take another look at our Problem-Handling Model on page 119 of your *Parent's Guide.*

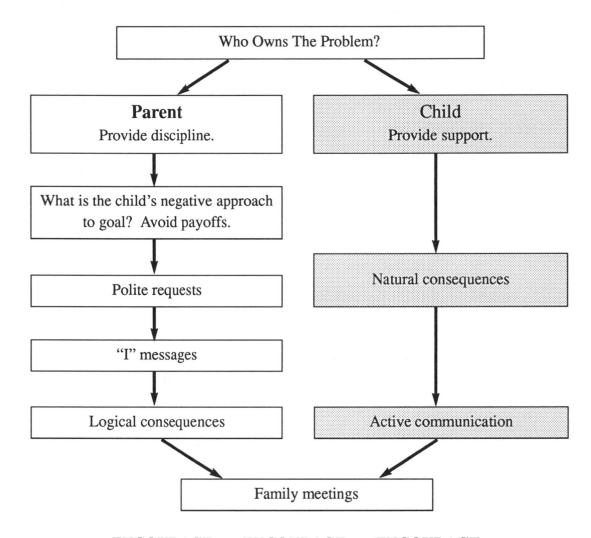

```
                    ┌─────────────────────────┐
                    │   Who Owns The Problem?  │
                    └─────────────────────────┘
```

Parent
Provide discipline.

Child
Provide support.

What is the child's negative approach to goal? Avoid payoffs.

Polite requests

Natural consequences

"I" messages

Logical consequences

Active communication

Family meetings

ENCOURAGE . . . ENCOURAGE . . . ENCOURAGE.

Last session we focused on the parent-owned problem side of the model, and how we could use discipline skills to teach responsibility. This week we'll be looking at the child-owned side of the model, and how we can use active communication to support our children in handling their own problems—thus teaching the value of cooperation in the process.

Let's watch a video that makes some very important points about this.

"The Brown Flower With The Green Stem"

 How does this story relate to parenting?

- We must allow our children the freedom to make some of their own decisions now if we want them to learn to make good decisions later.

No matter who owns the problem, children must be free to participate in problem handling, and when they own the problem, we must have the courage to let them decide how to handle it. Hopefully, they will allow us to participate.

Who owns the problem?

Parent	Child

- child participates
- parent decides how to solve

- parent participates
- child decides how to solve

Both require cooperation, but when we are supporting a child in handling a problem, we must rely on our ability to influence, not discipline. We have to have confidence that our children can handle the consequences of bad decisions and learn from their mistakes.

 Why is this critical, especially if they are to stay drug free later?

- Because we will not be around when they are offered drugs, we must prepare them to make good decisions on their own.
- This means letting them learn from mistakes that aren't as dangerous as drugs.

III. Communication (15 min. _____ to _____)

A. Types of Communication

The road to cooperation is communication.

 Communication

Now, we've all heard that word used in a number of settings, but to look at it more closely, how do we communicate?

- words
- tone of voice
- body language

When we have a problem and people are using words, tone and body language that are positive and accepting, what happens?

- We want to share with them, we want their support.

But when people are using words, tone and body language that are negative, judgmental and discouraging, what do we want to do?

- avoid them, not share our problems

Most people think that words carry most of the message. In fact, most communication experts say the following:

- body (and face)   most
- tone   much
- words   some

That's why we can use words that are not so negative but still turn our children off. Our tone of voice and body language are giving a very different message from the words. This is what we call a "mixed message."

B. Mixed Messages Activity

To get a feel for how mixed messages can confuse children, let's try an activity. First, find a partner.
(Once everyone is paired . . .)

Words: "I'm not angry; you can do whatever you like."

Now, I'd like one of you to say these words to the other, but let your tone of voice say this:

Tone of voice: "I'm really *very* angry, and if you don't do what I want, it's going to get even worse!"

Any questions? Okay, try it and see how it feels.
(Allow about 30 seconds.)

 What was that like for you? What did you think? How did you feel in either role?
(Allow brief discussion, focusing on feelings of confusion and being manipulated.)

Let's try saying the same line, only this time let your words and your tone say you're *not* angry, and let your body language and facial expression say the second line—you are *very* angry.

 Words and tone: "I'm not angry, you can do whatever you like."
Body and face: "I'm really *very* angry!"

(Allow a few seconds.)

 What was it like for you this time?
(Allow sharing.)

What we are trying to get across in this section is the importance of having all three channels of communication deliver the same message. This may mean a little attitude adjustment on your part, so you really think and feel what you are saying.

C. Communication Blocks

This will also help you achieve one of our goals in *Active Parenting Today*—helping you become what is called an "askable parent."

 Askable parent

This is the kind of parent a child will come to with a problem to ask for support.

 Notes _____
_____
_____
_____
_____
_____

What kinds of qualities do you look for in friends in order to feel comfortable asking them for support in problem situations?

 (Board their suggestions. Here are some examples:)

- trusting
- accepting
- nonjudgmental
- encouraging
- helpful

 And what qualities turn you off to talking about your problems? What might block communication?

- judging
- being sarcastic
- psychologizing
- being a know-it-all

We call these Communication Blocks, and the first step in being an effective communicator is to avoid blocking communication. Let's take a look at some examples of how parents block communication, so we'll know what to avoid.

Communication Blocks

 Communication Blocks

- commanding
- interrogating
- being sarcastic
- advising
- distracting

- moralizing
- placating
- psychologizing
- being a know-it-all

 What happened to the relationship between Janelle and her parents when they used communication blocks?

- They lost touch.

Since we all have our pitfalls as parents in terms of communication blocks, it's a good idea for us to take a look at some of the personal blocks we use.

D. Communication Blocks Activity

(Divide into groups of 4 or 5.)

Think about the Communication Blocks you tend to use most often. Then on page 136 of your *Parent's Guide*, jot them down. Also indicate the usual situations and what you see as your intention for using those blocks.

PG 136

Block   Situation   Intention

Here is where your courage comes in, because it isn't easy for us to look at ourselves and our actions when we may be making mistakes.

Let me give you an example:
(Give a personal example if possible.)

_____

_____

_____

_____

For example, a father learned his son didn't get a part he wanted in the school play. The son told his father about it, expressing a lot of pain and disappointment.

The father felt so badly for his son that he distracted him by talking about the camping trip they were planning.

If the father were to fill in the spaces, he would probably write this:

Block	Situation	Intention
Distracting	Son didn't get the part in the school play.	To make him feel better—so I'd feel better.

What's wrong with wanting to make your children feel better?

- It denies their right to own their feelings.
- It says, "I don't think you have the courage to handle feeling bad for a little while."

This activity will help you get in touch with your own thinking and the feelings that motivate the blocking responses.

- **Remember, just fill in the blocks you commonly use since we all use some of them occasionally.**
- **Take a minute to record your examples. Then I'll ask you to discuss them with your group members.**

(After 1 or 2 minutes, ask them to discuss their "blocks"; allow a few minutes.)

 Okay, what did you learn?
(Encourage sharing.)

When we come back from our break in 10 minutes, we'll explore some communication skills for winning cooperation with your children.

 Break (10 min. _____ to _____)

Notes _____

_____

_____

_____

_____

_____

_____

_____

_____

_____

_____

_____

IV. Active Communication (45 min. _____ to _____)

A. Five Steps

In order to become an askable parent and win our children's cooperation, we'll not only want to avoid blocking communication, but to also be a positive influence with our communication. To help us do that is a 5-step process called Active Communication.

Let's look at the 5 steps in the Active Communication process:

Active Communication
1. Listen actively.
2. Listen for feelings.
3. Connect feelings to content.
4. Look for alternatives and evaluate consequences.
5. Follow up.

Let's start looking at these skills that encourage children to seek parental cooperation for problem solving.

1. Listen actively.

How do you know when people are listening to what you're saying?

- good eye contact
- acknowledge what you say
- nod their heads
- identify with your experiences
- full attention

Active listening incorporates all the answers you gave.

Active listening contains 3 major elements:

- **Attention:** This is accomplished by giving the child your undivided attention. Let the child know your focus is on what he is saying.

- **Acknowledgment:** The gestures and verbal responses such as "yes" and "uh-huh" indicate you understand what is being said.

- **Empathy:** Allow yourself to feel some of what your child is feeling, and to indicate through tone of voice and facial expression that you are experiencing the impact of what is being said. In short, you are listening for the feelings beneath the words your child is saying.

 Any questions or comments about Step 1: Listen actively?

Okay, let's look at the heart of the Active Communication process, Steps 2 and 3.

When our children have a problem, we usually focus on what happened—the "content"—and ignore the child's feelings about what happened. Steps 2 and 3 of Active Communication are to listen for the feelings about the problem and then to help the child connect those feelings to the problem.

 Children don't care how much you know until they know how much you care.

 Why is it important to "listen for feelings" and to connect them to content? (Many answers are correct:)

- It helps children feel our support.
- It helps them learn how to communicate feelings with words rather than misbehavior.
- It helps us learn what children are really thinking behind their words.

 Notes _____

_____

_____

_____

_____

_____

_____

_____

_____

_____

_____

_____

_____

_____

Once we've established an open line of communication by focusing on our child's feelings and listening actively, we can help the child begin to look for a solution. This is Step 4: Look for alternatives and help the child evaluate the possible consequences of those alternatives.

 It's really important to take a "palms up" type of posture (show a palms up gesture), to say something, like, "I don't know what you'll decide to do." Can you tell me why this is important?

- Since the child owns responsibility for the problem, it's only fair she be allowed to decide what course of action to take. If we come on too strong, she'll back off. The palms up position, both literally and figuratively, helps let her know that we're only a consultant in this. The child has the real decision-making power.

Later, after the child has had a chance to put her decision into practice, we can ask her how it went. This is Step 5: Follow up. If it didn't go well, we can begin the process over again.

Let's take a look at an example of the Active Communication process as demonstrated by Pat and Janelle. As you watch, see if you can remember where Pat uses the 5 steps. (The 5 steps should be visible during the video.)

《 # 4 》 Active Communication

• •

That was a lot more satisfying, wasn't it? Let's see how Pat did it.

 First, how did she "listen actively"—the first step in Active Communication?

- She gave Janelle her undivided attention.
- She acknowledged what Janelle was saying.
- She seemed empathetic—caring.

 PG 131-132 Now, before we go through the other 4 steps, I'd like you to turn to pages 131 and 132 in your *Parent's Guide*. You'll find a copy of the dialogue between Pat and Janelle. Please take a few minutes to go through and indicate when Pat uses each of the 4 remaining steps. Circle the feeling words used; underline the words indicating when Pat connects feelings to content; put brackets around

dialogue showing when she helps Janelle look for alternatives and evaluate consequences; and write "follow-up" in the left-hand margin beside dialogue when Pat finds out how it went.

- circle - feeling words
- underline - connect feelings to content
- bracket - alternatives and consequences
- write in margin - "follow-up"

(Allow 3-4 minutes as necessary. Refer to the dialogue on the following page for guidance as you ask about each step.)

What feeling words did Pat use to indicate she was "listening for feelings," Step 2?

Were there any times when Pat connected feelings to the content of what happened?

How did Pat use Step 4, "Look for alternatives and evaluate consequences," to help Janelle develop problem-solving skills?

What did Pat do for Step 5, "Follow-up"?

Notes _____
_____
_____
_____
_____
_____
_____
_____
_____
_____
_____
_____
_____
_____
_____

Active Communication Dialogue

Janelle: I don't believe it!

Pat: You don't believe what?

Janelle: Mrs. Hickman. I was sitting there minding my own business while Denise and Cathy keep whispering to me about this birthday party, and I told them I was going but to please be quiet. Then Mrs. Hickman looks up and sees me whispering to Denise to be quiet and thinks I'm the one who was talking and gave me extra homework because I 'apparently have so much time on my hands I don't know what to do.' It isn't fair.

Pat: You sure sound angry.

Janelle: Yes. Wouldn't you? I mean, I didn't even want to be talking!

Pat: And yet you're the one who got in trouble. I can see why you'd be upset.

Janelle: And to make matters worse, Denise and Cathy didn't say a word. They just sat there and giggled.

Pat: You must have been furious about that.

Janelle: I'll say! They started it, and then let me take all the blame!

Pat: And, of course, all Mrs. Hickman saw was you talking.

Janelle: Right. So she thinks it's all my fault.

Pat: I guess you were a little embarrassed too, when she called you down in front of the whole class.

Janelle: Yeah. But the other kids saw what was going on, so it wasn't that bad. But now I have all this homework to do. Well, it's not fair. I'm not going to do it.

Pat: [That's one thing you could do. What would happen if you didn't do it?]

Janelle: I guess she'd give me an "F" to average in with my grades.

Pat: Ouch! That could really hurt especially after all the hard work you've put in. [What else could you do?]

Janelle: I could tell what really happened?

Pat: [Yes, you could. What do you think would happen then?]

> **Janelle:** Well . . . the other kids would probably put me down for being a tattletale, and Mrs. Hickman would just tell me I had no business talking anyway—that I should have ignored them.
>
> **Pat:** [What do you think about that?]
>
> **Janelle:** I guess it was pretty dumb. I mean, I guess I knew that she didn't allow talking at all. But Mom, I didn't want them to think I'm a snob.
>
> **Pat:** I see. You were afraid they wouldn't like you if you followed Mrs. Hickman's rules and kept quiet. So you let them get you in trouble because you wanted them to like you.
>
> **Janelle:** Yeah. Pretty dumb, wasn't it?
>
> **Pat:** Well . . . let's put it this way: It's only dumb if you keep doing it. It may be a mistake you can learn something from.
>
> A few days later. . .
>
> **Pat:** Oh, Janelle. I've been meaning to ask—how did that whispering in class thing work out? Did you do the extra homework?
>
> **Janelle:** Yeah. I didn't think an "F" would be too great.
>
> **Pat:** And how about Denise and Cathy? They still getting you to talk during class?
>
> **Janelle:** No way! I told them I didn't like what they did, and that the next time I was going to ignore them.
>
> **Pat:** Attagirl. I like the way you stood up for yourself. It's smart not to let people take advantage of you.

Follow-up (first occurrence, beside "Pat: Oh, Janelle...")

Follow-up (second occurrence, beside "Pat: And how about Denise and Cathy?")

Notes _____

_____

_____

B. Responding to Feelings Video Practice

PG 138

Please turn to page 138 in your *Parent's Guide* for a Video Practice that will help us learn to listen for and respond to feelings—not just content. There are 10 short vignettes in this practice. After each I'll stop the tape for you to think of a feeling word and write down how you might use it in the parent response. (If time is tight, you might have parents write down only the feeling word for the first 5, then the entire response for the remaining 5.)

Let's try the first one.

140

Responding to Feelings Video Practice

● ●

(Play the first vignette, pausing on the child's expression.)

? **Ask yourself, what was Sara feeling? Then jot that feeling word and your parent response in the blank for Scene 1.**
(Allow a few seconds.)

? **What did you come up with?**

- feeling word: embarrassed
- parent's response: "That sure sounds embarrassing."

Let's try the next one.
(Play each scene, pausing the tape to allow parents to write a response; then discuss as above. Use the following guide sheet as a reference, but remember there may be other accurate responses as well.)

Scene	Child's Feeling	Parent's Response
1. Sara	embarrassed	"That sure sounds embarrassing."
2. Zack	hurt	"You sound hurt that he didn't invite you, too."
3. Ramon	angry	"You sure are angry at your sister."
4. Ben	scared	"I can see how scared you are."
5. Jade	bored	"I guess you're feeling pretty bored."
6. Janelle	proud	"You sound really proud of the way you handled that."
7. Sara	determined	"You're really determined to stand up for yourself."
8. Zack	irritated	"You're getting really irritated with your brother, aren't you?"
9. Ramon	overwhelmed	"You sound overwhelmed with all you have to do."
10. Jade	concerned	"You're really concerned about the planet."

C. Role-Playing Active Communication Activity

Nowhere is becoming an askable parent more important than in the area of drug prevention. When our children feel they can talk with us about tobacco, alcohol and other drugs safely—in other words, without our using Communication Blocks or other discouraging actions—then we have a chance to educate and influence them towards positive choices.

Let's practice our Active Communication skills with role-playing based on this important area. If your children aren't old enough to be dealing with these issues now, they soon will be.

Please get a partner and decide who will play the parent and who the child. (After everyone is paired . . .)
(Make sure the Active Communication steps are in view.)

For those of you playing the child, here's the situation: You are 11 years old, and a few of your friends have gotten some beer and want you to join them Saturday at a secret place to try it. You're curious about beer, but you know it isn't good for kids, and you don't really want to go. You're afraid they will think you're a chicken and won't do other things with you, either.

Your first line is this:

Child: "Can I talk to you about something?"

Parents, here's your job:

1. Listen actively.
2. Respond at least twice with feeling words.
3. Help the child look at alternatives and evaluate consequences.

One hint: You'll find feeling responses work better if you make them tentative. For example, avoid saying this:

"You are sad."

You might say:

"You sound sad."

or . . .

"I guess you're sad about that."

 Are there any questions?
(Clarify as needed.)

Okay, see what you come up with.
(Allow 3-5 minutes as needed, walking around the room to see how it is going. Then process, asking questions like the following:)

How did it go?

Did you respond to feelings?

What alternatives did you come up with?

Let's switch roles now so everyone has a chance to practice. We're going to make one change though. Sometimes children come to us with their concerns when they really have no decision to make. Sometimes they just need some accurate information. But if we only give them the information without responding to their feelings, it may fall on deaf ears. Remember:

Children don't care how much you know, until they know how much you care.

So this time your job as parents is slightly different:

    1. Listen actively.
    2. Respond at least twice with feeling words.
    3. Provide accurate information.

Here's the situation: Your 7-year-old child has heard so much about how "drugs can kill" that he is afraid to take doctor-prescribed medicine he needs for strep throat.

Use your modified Active Communication skills to help.
(After 3-5 minutes, process as before.)

V. Family Enrichment Activity: Bedtime Routines And I Love You's (7 min. _____ to _____)

It's once again time for our Family Enrichment Activity.

How many of you have ever had trouble getting your children to go to bed on time?

Well, this video may give you some ideas that will help. Of course, logical consequences, encouragement and your communication skills will also be important.

 Family Enrichment Activity: Bedtime Routines And I Love You's

. . . .

Any comments or questions about that vignette?

You'll find some tips for bedtime routines in your *Parent's Guide*, as well as a guide sheet for using them at home this week.

VI. Video Review (3 min. _____ to _____)

Before we end, let's review what we've covered this session.

 Video Review

. . . .

VII. Home Activities (2 min. _____ to _____)

Your Home Activities are listed in your *Parent's Guide* on page 139. We'll read over the list together.

144

HOME ACTIVITIES

1. **Read Chapter 5 in your *Parent's Guide* to reinforce what you've learned about communication. If you wish to read ahead, please do so.**
2. **Do the Family Enrichment Activity: Bedtime Routines And I Love You's, completing page 135.**
3. **Look for at least one opportunity to use Active Communication when your child owns a problem, and fill in the guide sheet on page 137.**
4. **Call your buddy (optional).**

Have a great week. And be here next week for graduation! I'll have your certificates and some more important skills for your parenting tool chest.

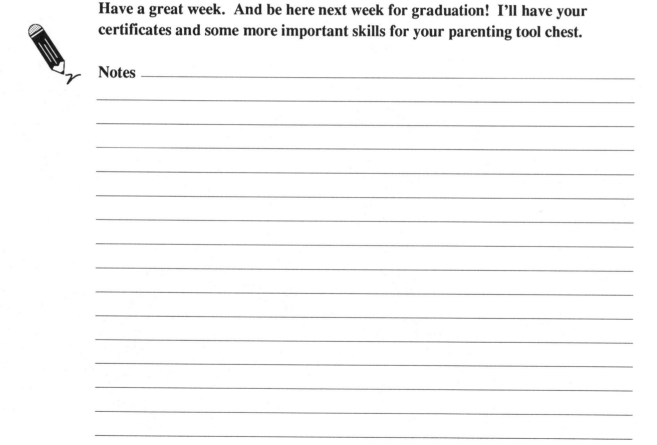

Notes _____

_____

_____

_____

_____

_____

_____

_____

_____

_____

_____

_____

_____

_____

_____

_____

_____

_____

SESSION 6

ACTIVE PARENTING IN A DEMOCRATIC SOCIETY

	Topic	Activity	Video
I	Share And Tell	Goal Card Review (optional)	
II	Family Talks		1. Family Talks (6:38)
III	Problem-Solving Discussions	Role Play: Problem Solving (optional)	2. Problem-Solving Discussions (5:51)
IV	The Family Council Meeting		3. The Family Council Meeting (6:05)
V	Accepting Problems as a Part of Family Living		4. "The Bumps" (1:34) 5. Share And Tell (3:30)
VI	What's Next?	Problem Solving	6. Video Review (:46)
VII	Closing	Encouragement	7. Family Enrichment Activity: Emphasizing The Family Unit (5:03)
VIII	Completing Your Experience as a Leader		

OBJECTIVES FOR SESSION 6:

- Build on the positive changes made during the program.
- Be able to hold a Family Talk using prevention of tobacco, alcohol and other drugs as an example.
- Be able to hold a family Problem-Solving Discussion using the 5 steps of active problem solving.
- Understand the procedure for holding a Family Council Meeting.
- Determine how participants might continue to build on their *Active Parenting Today* experience.

I. Share And Tell (30 min. _____ to _____)

A. Home Activities

Welcome to our final session of *Active Parenting Today*. Before we get into some exciting discussion techniques for your family, I want to spend some time reviewing what we've covered so far. Then, towards the end of our session, we'll have a chance to talk about where we might go from here.

  First, let's share a little about last week's Home Activities. Who had a success with the Family Enrichment Activity: "Bedtime Rituals And I Love You's"? You can turn in your *Parent's Guide* to page 135 to help jog your memory.

 Were there any problems or concerns that anyone wants to talk about?

Let's take a look at page 137 in the *Parent's Guide* and see how it went with your Active Communication assignment.

 Who would like to share?

 How about logical consequences or any of the other skills you have been using—how are things going?
(Allow time to problem solve difficult situations and brainstorm together.)

B. Goal Card Review Activity

(Pass out goal cards if you are using them.)

I'd like you to take a few minutes to complete your goal cards. Indicate your child's current levels of responsibility, cooperation, courage, self-esteem and any qualities you added on the grid, by placing a dot on the 1 to 10 scale, as you did during the first session.

(After they have done this . . .)

Now draw an arrow between the dots where your child was when we first did this and where your child is now, with the arrow pointing in the direction your child moved: to the right for progress and to the left if you saw a negative change.

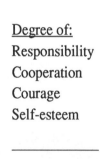 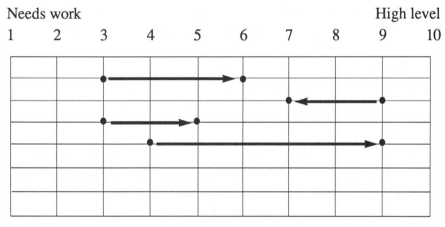

	Needs work								High level	
	1	2	3	4	5	6	7	8	9	10

Degree of:
Responsibility
Cooperation
Courage
Self-esteem

_____
_____
_____

 Let's use this information to think about the changes we have seen as a result of your efforts in this course. What has improved in your children's behavior, your own actions and the general atmosphere in your home?
(Encourage free sharing of outcomes.)

How many of you are now perfect parents and have perfect children to prove it?
(If they don't laugh, you're in trouble.)

How many of you still make mistakes as parents?

Great! Because what are mistakes for?

- learning

Right. Our goal in *Active Parenting Today* is not perfection. It's improvement. And as long as we are willing to accept responsibility for our mistakes and learn to make better choices in the future, we will continue to improve.

II. Family Talks (20 min. _____ to _____)

To set the stage for this topic, does anyone remember the first freedom protected by the U.S. Bill of Rights?
(When leading *Active Parenting Today* in a country other than the U.S., find examples from your own country's struggle for democracy.)

- freedom of speech

Right. Freedom of speech is at the core of democratic living. Let's watch our first video to see how this important concept impacts family living. Then we'll learn about 3 ways to apply this in your families.

- Family Talks
- Problem-Solving Discussions
- Family Council Meetings

 Family Talks

• •

Why do you suppose we used the subject of alcohol and other drugs as an example of how to hold a Family Talk?

- It's such an important area for parents to talk to their children about.

You saw in the video that Steve and Pat have made the decision to drink in moderation. This is both a legal decision and one that fits their family values. Many parents, however, choose not to drink at all, and they would want to share *this* value with their children.

Notes _____

_____

_____

_____

? **What are some reasons why families adopt a "no drinking" policy?**

- religious tradition
- history of alcoholism
- health reasons
- other _____
- _____
- _____

Regardless of *your* decision about drinking, we've all heard that parents should talk to their children about alcohol and other drugs. Tobacco is also a harmful substance you might want to discuss. But very seldom does anyone tell you *how* to have such a talk or what you might say. Let's go over some tips for having good Family Talks about this or any other topic. (▰ Then, if you would like a copy of the booklet that Steve and Pat gave Janelle in that vignette [hold up a copy], you can get one from me at the end of the session.)

 Tips for Family Talks

- Plan how you will introduce the topic.
- Think of questions that will stimulate discussion.
- Write down key points you want to make.
- Find support materials: a video, audio or print.

? **What age should children be for you to begin talking to them about tobacco, alcohol and other drugs?**

- With children as young as 5 or 6, you can talk briefly about "good drugs" (those the doctor prescribes and a parent gives you) and "bad drugs."

Notes _____

_____

_____

_____

_____

_____

_____

_____

_____

Because we would like you to have a Family Talk about alcohol and other drugs at home, let's use that as an example to plan a Family Talk.

 Please turn in your *Parent's Guide* to page 156. Let's review how Steve and Pat handled these tips as you plan for your own Family Talk. You can write down their examples or modify them to fit your own style.

 First, how did Steve introduce the topic?

- After introducing the idea of Family Talks, he says:

    "I'm sure you've heard a lot about alcohol and other drugs, and how messed up some kids are getting on them."

    "So we thought our first Family Talk could be about alcohol and other drugs. How does that sound to you?"

 What are some ways you would be comfortable bringing up the subject with your children?
(Allow some sharing.)

 Now take a minute to write a brief introduction in the space provided in your *Parent's Guide*.
(Allow 1 or 2 minutes, offering help if anyone needs it.)

 What about the second tip: What were some questions Pat and Steve asked Janelle to keep the talk going? And as we talk, be sure to jot down questions you might ask in a Family Talk at home.

- Steve asked her what she had learned about drugs in school.
- Pat asked if they told her why drugs were bad for her.
- Pat asked why she thought people used drugs.

 What were some points they made about alcohol and other drugs? Again, be sure to make notes about the points you want to cover—if you choose to use alcohol and other drugs as the topic.

- A lot of kids get messed up using drugs.
- They often lead to dropping out and failure.
- They can damage the brain—especially in children and teens.

- No one should use illegal drugs.
- Adults should only use legal drugs in moderation—if they choose to use them at all.
- Drug use can lead to addiction.
- Drugs may make you feel good now, but they make you feel a lot worse later.

Finally, what support material did Steve and Pat use?

- a booklet

What support materials would you use?
(This is a good time to introduce other resources or brainstorm with the group.)

Have any of you already had this type of Family Talk at home?

How did it go?
(Try to bring out the positive to encourage the others to have a prevention talk at home this week if appropriate.)

Break   (10 min. _____ to _____)

III. Problem-Solving Discussions (20 min. _____ to _____)

A. Active Problem-Solving Process

You might have noticed in the last vignette that Janelle mistakenly thought a Family Talk might be a time to discuss problems. We've seen that Family Talks are about topics and not about conflicts and problem solving. There is another type of discussion that is designed for these situations. Turn in your _Parent's Guide_ to page 157.

You'll notice a technique called a Problem-Solving Discussion. The Problem-Solving Discussion can be done by itself or as part of a complete Family Council Meeting, which we'll see in a few minutes.

Notes _____

_____

"Democracy doesn't mean you always get your way; it means you always get your say."

We heard this quote by Dr. Popkin earlier. What does this concept of freedom of speech have to do with *Active Parenting Today*?

- We are raising children to thrive in the society in which they'll live.
- In a representative democracy, our leaders make the laws and decisions by which we live.
- We can influence their decisions through discussion—free speech.
- Without free speech, rebellion is the only way people can influence those decisions.
- It's the same in a family: We can either allow our children ways to influence our decisions through discussion, or they will eventually rebel against our dictatorship and undermine our authority.

Now, let's see how a Problem-Solving Discussion works.

Problem-Solving Discussions

Active Problem Solving

1. Clearly identify the problem.
2. Share thoughts and feelings.
3. Brainstorm possible solutions.
4. Decide on a solution.
5. Put decision into action.

Are there any questions about these steps or the active problem-solving process? (Discuss as necessary.)

Consensus

What does making a decision by "consensus" mean?

- You keep discussing alternative solutions until one is found that everyone can live with. It may not be anyone's first choice, but it's acceptable to all.

What if a consensus cannot be reached?

- The parent, as the leader in the family, may need to make a temporary decision until the matter can be brought up again in another session.

 ## B. Role-Play: Problem-Solving Activity

(Divide the group into families, having participants play father, mother and one or more children. They can decide what ages.)

(Provide a problem for them to use in practicing the active problem-solving process. For example, where to go on Sunday afternoon for a family outing or a conflict between two children over use of the TV. Allow 5-10 minutes to come up with a decision, then discuss how they used the 5 steps.)

 Notes _____

_____

_____

IV. The Family Council Meeting (10 min. ____ to ____)

 The Family Council Meeting is a regularly scheduled meeting that allows all family members a chance to actively participate in running the family.

There are many ways to hold a Family Council Meeting. We're going to see an example of one that uses the following agenda:

 Family Council Meeting
Agenda

1. Compliments
2. Reading the minutes
3. Old business/new business
4. Allowances
5. Treat or family activity

Let's take a look.

The Family Council Meeting

PG | 150-153

 Are there any comments or questions about the Family Council Meeting or the agenda on the board?
(Help clarify any questions, referring the group to pages 150 to 153 in the *Parent's Guide* for more details on how to hold a meeting.)

What is the purpose of posting an agenda on the refrigerator or other common area?

- So that anyone with a problem or conflict can easily add it to the agenda for the next meeting. This assures everyone that his or her needs and concerns will be heard.

If you'd like to try a Family Council Meeting at home this week, you might try a simple Problem-Solving Discussion during the new business section. For example, decide on something the whole family can do together on Sunday afternoon—something fun! Keep the meeting short, and be sure to read your *Parent's Guide* for details.

V. Accepting Problems as a Part of Family Living

(10 min. _____ to _____)

One of the themes of *Active Parenting Today* has been that problems are not our enemies, they're our opportunities—opportunities to teach courage, self-esteem, responsibility, cooperation, problem-solving skills and a host of other qualities.

 Let's watch our final teaching story as Laura introduces this idea to her boys.

Notes _____

_____

_____

_____

_____

_____

"The Bumps"

 Mistakes are for learning.

Opportunities, not enemies.

The bumps are what we climb on.

 What does this story mean to you in terms of your family and your parenting?
(Allow brief discussion, making sure you or someone makes the following point.)

Problems are a natural part of family living, and though we hope this _Active Parenting Today_ course will help reduce the problems in your family, there will always be problems. The key is how you handle them.

Now, let's have our final visit with the Davidson family.

 ## Share And Tell

 Any thoughts or comments about the Davidsons?

 # VI. What's Next? (10 min. _____ to _____)

A. Problem-Solving Activity

In the last vignette, Diane mentioned that her group has decided to continue to meet once a month. I thought we might have a short Problem-Solving Discussion together to see what you can do to continue your progress.

 1. The problem: What's next?
2. Sharing

Since Step 2 is for sharing, does anyone have thoughts or feelings about continuing to build on your progress in *Active Parenting Today* and keep from backsliding?

(Postpone any suggestions to Step 3.)

Let's do some brainstorming to see what kind of possibilities we can come up with.

(Board as they suggest, including any courses such as *Family Talk* or *Windows* that you might like to get going. Other ideas include:)

3. Brainstorming
    * Meet monthly for support and sharing.
    * Have a social event together and bring our families.
    * Use supplemental resources on our own and/or discuss in follow-up sessions.

(After a number of ideas are generated . . .)

Let's go to Step 4: Deciding. Which idea do you want to put into action?
(Try to come up with 1 or 2 ideas that most of the group will do.)

B. Video Review

Now, let's watch our final video review.

Video Review

VII. Closing (10 min. _____ to _____)

A. Encouragement Activities

(If you have time, one of these two encouragement activities can help you end on a very positive note.)

Option 1. "Buddy Share"

(Have parents pair up with their buddies and spend a minute each, sharing what strengths and progress they have seen their buddies make over this course, what they have gotten from their buddies and what they appreciate.)

- Strengths
- Progress
- Appreciation

 Option 2. "Pats on The Back in Writing"

(This takes a little longer, but provides a nice keepsake of the course. Hand each person an 8 1/2" x 11" sheet of paper—card stock weight is best—and a piece of tape. Ask them to help tape the sheet to each person's back. The instructions are to mill around the room writing encouraging comments on anyone's paper with whom you would like to share a strength, an area of progress or an appreciation. Using their *Parent's Guide* as a backing to put under the paper as they go around will make it easier to write. You can limit the time as needed.)

B. Family Enrichment Activity: Emphasizing The Family Unit

 Family Enrichment Activity: Emphasizing The Family Unit

HOME ACTIVITIES

1. Read Chapter 6.
2. Complete the Family Enrichment Activity: Emphasizing The Family Unit.
3. Have a Problem-Solving Discussion as part of a Family Council Meeting or by itself, completing the guide sheet on page 157.
4. Have a Family Council Meeting, completing page 158.
5. Have a Family Talk about tobacco, alcohol and other drugs using the optional booklet *Active Parenting Family Guide: Tobacco, Alcohol and Other Drugs* if appropriate.
6. Remember that "mistakes are for learning." Be forgiving of yourself and continue to practice all your *Active Parenting Today* skills. Encourage, encourage, encourage yourself!

(This is a place to write your own closing, perhaps building on the last video. You might share a poem or other inspirational material.)

_____

_____

_____

_____

_____

(If you have evaluations, pass them out. Then, if you are using Parent Completion Certificates, award them.)

This concludes our _Active Parenting Today_ group. The parenting education movement continues to grow because parents like you tell other parents about your course. If this was a worthwhile experience for you, and I sincerely hope it was, please tell your friends about our next _Active Parenting Today_ group.

_____

_____

_____

(Note: Many groups like to end with a party or refreshments.)

VIII. Completing Your Experience as a Leader

Completion of any worthwhile task is important. To help you complete this experience of leading an Active Parenting group, we recommend 3 steps. In addition, if you choose, we would appreciate hearing about your experience. You might send us copies of any special evaluations you received, or your own anecdotes and thoughts.

Step 1: What did you like about how you led the group?

_____

_____

_____

_____

_____

Step 2: What will you do differently next time?

_____

_____

_____

_____

_____

_____

Step 3: You have just made an important contribution to the lives of several families. Acknowledge that contribution and allow yourself to feel good about it. Because the future of humankind is its children and teens, the key to that future rests on the quality of parenting they receive. Your contribution to that future, to repeat the words of Emerson quoted in the introduction to this guide, is part of your own success.

Congratulations on your success!

Notes _____

_____

_____

_____

_____

_____

_____

_____

_____

_____

_____

_____

_____

_____

_____

_____

_____

Notes

The poem "Flowers" written by Michael H. Popkin;

original watercolor painting by R. Scott Coleman

OSAP Roles for "Parent Training Is Prevention" of Alcohol And Other Drugs

The Office of Substance Abuse Prevention (OSAP) suggests these 10 roles that parents can play in the prevention of drug use.

1. Parents as role models.
Be a positive role model. Children learn best by example.

2. Parents as educators or information resources.
Be informed about tobacco, alcohol and other drugs, and share this with your child.

3. Parents as policy makers and rule setters.
Make a "no use" rule—"No use of illegal drugs by anyone in the family, and no use of alcohol or nicotine by anyone under the legal age"—and enforce it.

4. Parents as stimulators of and participants in healthy activities.
Encourage your child to take part in hobbies, school activities and sports. Get involved yourself; plan fun family activities.

5. Parents as consultants and educators on peer pressure.
"Just say no" is easier said than done. Teach your child how to resist peer pressure without him or her feeling foolish.

6. Parents as monitors and supervisors.
Set and enforce curfews; know where your children are.

7. Parents as collaborators with other parents.
Join with other parents to gain support and new ideas. There's strength in numbers.

8. Parents as identifiers and confronters of drug use.
Know how to identify drug use and confront your child when necessary.

9. Parents as managers of intoxicated children.
Get immediate medical help when your child is semi-conscious or unconscious or if you are in doubt.

10. Parents as managers of their own feelings.
Don't blow up; don't give up. You're not guilty.

References

Adler, A. (1920). *The Practice and Theory of Individual Psychology.* New York: Harcourt, Brace.

Ansbacher, H.L. & Ansbascher, R. (1964). *The Individual Psychology of Alfred Adler.* New York: Harper Torchbooks.

Dinkmeyer, D. & McKay, G. (1976). *Systematic Training for Effective Parenting.* Circle Pines, MN: American Guidance Service.

Dreikurs, R. & Stoltz, V. (1964). *Children: The Challenge.* Des Moines, IA: Meredith Press.

Ellis, A. (1962). *Reason and Emotion in Psychotherapy.* New York: Lyle Stuart.

Fine, M. (1989). *The Second Handbook on Parent Education.* San Diego: Academic Press.

Ginott, H. (1965). *Between Parent and Child.* New York: Macmillan.

Gordon, T. (1970). *Parent Effectiveness Training.* New York: Peter H. Wyden.

Popkin, M. (1983). *Active Parenting Action Guide.* Atlanta: Active Parenting.

Popkin, M. (1983). *Active Parenting Handbook.* Atlanta: Active Parenting.

Popkin, M. (1990). *Active Parenting of Teens Parent's Guide.* Atlanta, GA: Active Parenting.

Popkin, M. (1987). *Active Parenting: Teaching Cooperation, Courage and Responsibility.* San Francisco: Harper and Row, Publishing.

ACTIVE PARENTING PUBLISHERS TRAINING PROGRAMS

Leader Certification Workshop (LCWs)

Learn how you can make a difference in your community by attending a Leader Certification Workshop (LCW). You'll review the video-based sessions, enhance your group leadership skills and exchange ideas with fellow participants. You will also receive: a *Leader's Guide, Parent's Handbook, Promotion Guide* and Leader Certificate. Earn seven contact hours of continuing education credits. The $99 Early Bird Fee (Regular Price: $119) could be one of the best investments you'll ever make! To find out more about Active Parenting Publishers Leader Certification Workshops, call **1-800-825-0060, ext. LCW.** In Canada, call Al Reynar, c/o Active Parenting Canada, 403-526-4994.

Special Leader Certification Workshops

In addition to our regularly-scheduled Leader Certification Workshops, Active Parenting Publishers can design and implement a Special Leader Certification Workshop especially for your organization or group. If you have a minimum of 25 people, we'll send a trainer to conduct a Special Leader Certification Workshop at a location convenient to you. Call Karen Lindroth at **1-800-825-0060** for more information.

Training of Trainers (ToT) Seminars

Active Parenting Publishers Training of Trainers (ToT) seminars bring prominent helping professionals together at a scenic site to train and authorize a limited number of certified Active Parenting trainers to present Leader Certification Workshops for the following Active Parenting programs: *Active Parenting Today, Active Parenting of Teens, Windows* and *Free the Horses.* Our three-day ToT seminars feature presentations, problem-solving sessions and individual consultations. To ensure that our commitment to quality is achieved, ToT participants must have attended an LCW and led at least one group in the Active Parenting program for which they would like to receive ToT certification. Enrollment in our ToT seminars is limited to 60 participants. Register Today — your satisfaction is guaranteed! Call **1-800-825-0060, ext. ToT.**

ACTIVE PARENTING PUBLISHERS